BURKE
AND HARE

The True Story

HUGH DOUGLAS

ROBERT HALE & COMPANY

© *Hugh Douglas* *1973*
First published in Great Britain *1973*

ISBN 0 7091 3777 X

Robert Hale & Company
63 Old Brompton Road
London, S.W.7

MADE AND PRINTED IN GREAT BRITAIN BY
THE GARDEN CITY PRESS LIMITED
LETCHWORTH, HERTFORDSHIRE SG6 1JS

To my medical friends
JAMES BRUCE, GEORGE CARDNO
and in memory of
CHARLES THOMSON

CONTENTS

CONTENTS

ILLUSTRATIONS

PREFACE

> Up the close and doon the stair
> Ben the hoose wi' Burke and Hare,
> Burke's the butcher, Hare's the thief,
> Knox the boy who buys the beef.

Four scurrilous lines but an accurate enough summing up of the murders in the West Port of Edinburgh during 1827 and 1828. Mary Docherty, indeed, went up the close, and down the stair into the house of Burke and Hare. Fifteen others preceded her—some of them well-known figures in the city and others poor creatures whose names were not known to their murderers and who were hardly even missed.

"Burke's the butcher"—that is what the law said with absolute truth, but was Burke the only butcher?

"Hare's the thief"—there can be no doubt about that; but the house from which he stole was "the bloody house of life". Was he in fact a greater fiend than Burke as was commonly thought at the time or did he deserve the lesser punishment?

And "Knox the boy that buys the beef"—Robert Knox bought the 'beef' all right, but did he know where it came from? For more than a century Knox has been held to be as guilty as the two murderers, but at last people are beginning to ask whether he was not the victim of a campaign of hate generated by the ignorant mob and jealous rivals.

The West Port murders is the most famous murder case in Scottish legal history, and one which is still talked of in whispers. The story has become part of Scotland's legend; it has given a word to the language, and it has inspired such authors as Robert Louis Stevenson and Dylan Thomas.

The West Port murders are set against Edinburgh in its golden age when chivalry was high fashion and the arts were flourishing mightily, they involved the lowest and the highest classes; they shook to its foundations the smug establishment of the day, and they brought home to everyone the twilight slum city, which all knew existed side by side with the opulent New Town, but of which few spoke.

I have tried to gather together all the known facts and to reassess them against this background. Help has come from many sources, and I am grateful to all those who have assisted and encouraged me. The staff of the Edinburgh Room of Edinburgh Public Library carried the greatest burden, but assistance was given by staffs of the Scottish Record Office, the National Library of Scotland, the British Museum and the High Court of Justiciary. I have quoted from Isobel Rae's biography of Robert Knox by permission of the author, and from Dylan Thomas's film script *The Doctor and the Devils* by permission of the publishers, Messrs J. M. Dent.

Lastly I would thank my wife, my family and friends who have listened patiently as the tale of Burke and Hare has unfolded. Here is the whole story for them.

HD

ONE

The Incomparable Anatomist

By the 1820s Edinburgh's Golden Age was ending, but it was not yet over. The Scottish capital comprised a teeming medieval city clinging to the hill on which the Castle was built, and a beautiful New Town of geometrically-precise streets and squares which spread out to the north and south of the old town. The first classical terraces of this new Edinburgh were already half a century old in 1820, and the majority of the nobility, lawyers and merchants had moved to a more spacious life there. They still returned to the narrow streets and winding braes of the old city each day to conduct their business, for the tidy terraces had not yet been violated by shops, banks, courts or offices, but private life now centred on the drawing rooms of their New Town houses rather than in public taverns as had been the custom in the eighteenth century.

The glitter of the Golden Age tarnished quickly after 1815 when Napoleon's defeat brought nearly half a century of continuous war to a close. Terrible financial depression followed, and from then until 1832 trade was bad, food very dear, unemployment rife, and the city itself was far on the road to bankruptcy.

In that generation many of the rich turned poor, and the poor became poverty-stricken. Edinburgh society as a whole had become less coarse and less drunken, but for the poor life tended to become harder, and the only source of solace which they could afford was drink. Two Edinburghs now existed side by side: as the rich deserted for the New Town, the old 'lands' (as the tall blocks of flats were called) decayed. More and more people were

13

crammed into the old houses, some of which were now over three
centuries old, to live with hunger, disease and misery as their
constant companions. The rich and the poor had once lived side
by side in these 'lands' so that neighbourliness cut across classes:
by the 1820s only the poor lived there, and cold charity had taken
the place of friendly interest. Edinburgh was not a city in which
to be poor.

During the long drawn-out French wars Scotland had been
isolated from Europe, and this resulted in a burgeoning of her
native artistic talents—architecture, painting, learning and literature blossomed so profusely that the frost of depression in the
post-war years could not destroy all the blooms. Improvements
continued to be effected, some planned, and some accidental. The
building of the Bridges destroyed many old tenements, and two
great fires in 1824 swept away almost every building on one side
of the High Street between St Giles and the Tron Church. The
Heart of Midlothian was removed in 1817, and the tidy minds
which had planned the New Town ruined the appearance of St
Giles and Parliament House by 'improvements' which spoiled their
original character. Not all the changes were bad: the removal of
the luckenbooths, or lock-up shops which clung like barnacles to
the walls of St Giles, was undoubtedly a change for the better.

Building alterations were not the only signs of Edinburgh's
continued progress in these difficult times. Princes Street was lit
by gas for the first time, the Union Canal linking the city with
Glasgow was opened, the Royal Scottish Academy was established,
and Scotland once again found her nationhood through Sir Walter
Scott, who lived the life of a laird and wrote novels which evoked
Scotland's past. It was he who rediscovered the Crown Jewels of
Scotland after they had been lost for a century; it was he who
brought the great cannon Mons Meg back to Scotland after it had
lain in the Tower of London for many years; and it was he who
stage-managed the visit of King George IV to Edinburgh in 1822,
the first time a reigning monarch had set foot in the Scottish
capital since the seventeenth century. The visit settled the differ-
ences between Scotland and England which had lingered since
the defeat of Prince Charles Edward Stuart at Culloden in 1746,

and it did this so successfully that the king himself appeared in full Highland dress—Stuart tartan, broadsword and pistols—and toasted the health of the clan chiefs.

With Scott at the peak of his powers, the city attracted great men of letters and music. Shelley, George Borrow, Southey, William Cobbett, Mendelssohn and Paganini all visited Edinburgh at that time.

In education, too, the period brought great advances. The ancient High School moved from its cramped quarters in the High School Wynd to a fine classical building designed by William Burn to sit on the edge of the Calton Hill, and a number of new schools— including Edinburgh Academy—were founded. The university, too, was expanding. It had now moved into new buildings on the South Bridge, and was attracting some of the finest scholars among its teachers, and great men of the future among its students. Charles Darwin was a student in Edinburgh between the years 1825 and 1827.

Without doubt the faculty of the University which was becoming most renowned was that of medicine. As in London and Dublin the process had begun in Edinburgh at the end of the seventeenth century when Alexander Menteith petitioned to be allowed to open a school of anatomy in the city, and to receive bodies for dissection. Throughout the eighteenth century and the early part of the nineteenth century the teaching of anatomy at Edinburgh University was in the hands of one family, the Alexander Monros—father, son and grandson—who taught there from 1705 to 1846.

The first two Alexander Monros were brilliant men who pushed Edinburgh to the forefront as a centre for the teaching of anatomy, but the third lacked the fire of his predecessors. He was content to read his grandfather's notes without changing so much as a phrase. "When I was a student in Leyden in 1719", he would say to his students although he was not even born in 1719. No wonder students began to drift away from the official classes to attend private lectures given by John Barclay, a man who was the exact antithesis of Monro. Barclay was full of fire and zeal, and a brilliant and spell-binding lecturer. He soon built up a huge class of three hundred students, and had to deliver his lectures twice a day to accommodate them. Other private schools opened in competition, but Barclay's was unique because the students saw in their tutor a dedicated lecturer who worked with them constantly and whose vast knowledge was available to them when they called upon it. That could not be said of many other anatomy lecturers, especially the aloof Alexander Monro.

In the year 1813 Barclay had in his class a young student who up to then had not been very successful in medicine, but who was to become one of the most famous—and notorious—anatomists of all time. His name was Robert Knox.

Knox was born in 1793, the eighth child of Robert Knox, a teacher of Natural Philosophy and Mathematics at George Heriot's School and his wife Mary. His father came from a line of stolid Kirkcudbright farmers and his mother was of German extraction, and from both Robert inherited tenacity, which he was going to need through much of his life.

As a child Robert contracted smallpox. Because of this illness Robert received his early education from his father, and he was 12 when he went on to the High School which was run at that time by Dr Alexander Adam, one of the school's most famous rectors. There Robert received as fine a classical education as the school could give, and when he left in 1810 he was Dux and Gold Medallist.

Robert chose medicine as a career, and began his studies at Edinburgh University that autumn. For three years he studied, but when he came to take his finals he failed—of all subjects— anatomy. The fault no doubt lay more in Monro's teaching than in Robert's ability, and it was then that he joined Dr Barclay's class for a year to help him to obtain his degree.

Like so many of his countrymen before and after, the newly-graduated doctor took the high road to London, where he continued his studies at St Bartholemew's Hospital until the French war broke out again early in 1815 and he joined the army as a hospital assistant. Knox was gazetted just two days before the Battle of Waterloo, and after the battle he was sent to Brussels where he spent several harrowing weeks among the wounded. He returned to England, but soon was sent abroad again—this time to the Cape of Good Hope, where he spent his spare time exploring and studying the people and animals. Towards the end of his stay at the Cape Knox was involved in a dispute with a Boer officer, which resulted in his being censured by a court of enquiry and horsewhipped by a settler. He made his undignified exit from the Cape towards the end of 1820.

Knox now returned to Edinburgh, but did not remain there long before he was off to Paris to continue his anatomical studies. In 1822 he came back to Edinburgh and set about building a career as a teacher of anatomy. He dissected diligently, he wrote learned papers, he set up a museum for the Royal College of Surgeons of Edinburgh, and he joined his old teacher Dr Barclay who now had an anatomy school at No 10 Surgeons' Square. In 1825 Knox became Barclay's partner, and when the old man died the following year, Knox inherited the most successful private anatomy school in Edinburgh.

Knox was a brilliant teacher. He started off with a great disadvantage, for the attack of smallpox in his childhood had left him with a most off-putting cadaverous appearance and a blind eye which gave rise to the nickname 'Old Cyclops'. He compensated for this by dressing showily and adopting a careful and graceful manner, which many mistook for vanity. He spoke eloquently and captured the attention and affection of his students whom he knew by their christian names. His biographer described his relationship with his students thus:

> When Knox sat down to instruct a pupil it was in a masterly fashion; the fine sweep of the scalpel, the line of precision, the unfolding of tissues, and finally a clear demonstration with a fund of information, physiological, surgical and pathological. When he saw a pupil slashing away at the muscles of a part, he touched the young man's shoulder and said, 'Ah, sir! I see you are dissecting for the sake of the bones; would it not be as well to pick up a few facts as to the attachments and uses of these muscles before you reach the skeleton?'

Knox inherited success from Barclay: now he increased it to

17

embarrassing proportions. Barclay had three hundred students and lectured twice a day, but Knox's roll grew to five hundred and he had to deliver his lectures three times. Yet he found time to give additional lectures which attracted doctors from far and wide, to run the museum of the Royal College of Surgeons of Scotland, and to lead a full social life at No 4 Newington Place. The only blot on his life was a secret marriage to 'a person of inferior rank', but he kept his wife out of his public life.

As he built up an army of admirers in his anatomy school Knox also made enemies. His political views tended to be radical and his scientific opinions were in advance of his times, so it was natural that the establishment should distrust him. His phenomenal success as a lecturer and his acid tongue on the subject of the competence of his colleagues in the medical profession also made him many enemies. It was natural enough that others who ran schools of anatomy—men like James Syme, John Lizars and John Aitken—should be jealous of his success, but Knox turned that envy into searing hatred which they were to direct on him later.

A malicious story attributed to one of his pupils gives an example of this. He began his lecture one day with a lengthy attack on Robert Liston for mistaking an aneurism for an abscess and lancing it with the result that the patient died. He ended his dissertation on the affair with the words: "It is surely unnecessary for me to add that a knowledge of anatomy, physiology and surgery is neither connected with nor dependent upon brute force, ignorance and presumption; nor has it anything to do with an utter destitution of honour and common honesty."

In 1827, however, it appeared as if nothing his rivals might do could dislodge him from the mountainpeak of success on which he stood. Robert Knox was at the summit of his career.

Knox advertised his course at the beginning of the season with an assurance to intending students that arrangements had been made "to secure as usual an ample supply of Anatomical Subjects", and that promise was not easily honoured. Obtaining subjects was a problem as old as anatomical dissection itself, and in Britain it was even more difficult than on the Continent. Anatomy schools in Europe were generally licensed and the supply of bodies for dissection was carefully regulated so that each had sufficient for its needs. In Britain, however, anyone could give lectures in anatomy, and the only subjects provided by law for dissection were the bodies of executed criminals. The supply was never adequate, and anatomists always had to augment it by robbing graves.

Grave-robbing began long before anatomy was organised as a regular subject in the University of Edinburgh. A manuscript dating from February 1678 refers to the stir caused by the resurrection of one of four gypsies who had been executed for murder and buried in Greyfriars Kirkyard. The story relates: "This four being throwen all into an hole digged for them in the Greyfrier Churchyard, with their clothes on; the next morning the youngest of the three sons (who was scarce 16), his body was missed and found to be away. Some thought he being the last throwen over the ladder, and first cut downe, and in full vigour, and no great heap of earth, and lying uppermost, and not so ready to smother, the fermentation of the blood and heat of the bodies under him, might cause him to rebound, and throw off the earth, and recover ere the morning and steal away; which, if true, he deserves his life, tho' the magistrates deserve a reprimande; but others more probably thought his body was stolen away by some chirurgien or his servant, to make ane anatomicale dissection on; which was criminal to take at their own hande, since the magistrates would not have refused it, and I hear the chirurgeons afferme, the town of Edinburgh is obliged to give them a malefactor's body once a year for that effect."

Worse was to follow: by the beginning of the eighteenth century there were scandals and riots in Edinburgh over the despoiling of graves in Greyfriars and other churchyards. In 1711 the minutes of the College of Surgeons in Edinburgh recorded: "Of late there has been a violation of sepulchres in the Grey Friars Churchyard, by some who most unchristianly have been stealing, or at least attempting to carry away the bodies of the dead out of their graves." Ten years later the College ordered surgeons' apprentices not to violate graves.

In 1742 a grave was discovered to have been disturbed in the West Kirkyard and a body was found soon afterwards near the shop of a surgeon called Martin Eccles. The mob quickly collected and proceeded to smash Eccles's shop to show their disgust at this violation of the dead. It was soon after this that a body was found in a sedan chair near the same spot, and the authorities assumed that it was on its way to the dissecting room, so the chairman and his assistant were banished from the city and the chair was burned by the hangman. A gardener, one John Samuel, was found trying to sell the body of a child who had been buried outside the city the day before, and was whipped through the streets and banished from Scotland for seven years.

The business had its lighter side, too. When Maggie Dickson was executed at Musselburgh a band of students tried to cut her body down and take it away for dissection, but her friends resisted and a pitched battle followed to gain possession of it. In the midst of the fight the 'body' suddenly came to life, for the hangman had only half-done his job, and Maggie was not dead at all. Indeed, she lived for another thirty years, and ever after was known as 'half-hangit' Maggie Dickson.

Murder for profit was not unknown. About the middle of the eighteenth century Ellen Terrence and her friend Jean Waldy met a poor woman with a little boy in the street, and one of the pair plied the woman with drink while the other enticed the boy into another room and smothered him. The body was sold to students for two shillings, plus another sixpence for carrying it to the anatomy rooms. After further bargaining the pair were given another tenpence to buy a dram. The murder was discovered, and both Terrence and Waldy were executed and dissected.

Even the worst criminals won sympathy when it came to dissection, for this was regarded as a terrible indignity, worse by far than execution itself. William Smith, who was sentenced to death in 1750 spoke for many when he made his plea:

As to my corporal frame, I know it is unworthy of material notice, but for the sake of that reputable family from which I am descended, I cannot refrain from anxiety, when I think how easily this poor body, in my friendless and necessitous condition, may fall into possession of the surgeons, and perpetuate my disgrace beyond the severity of the law.

Students had to hire guards to enable them to recov[...] from the gallows, and riots were frequent. At times thi[...] far as vengeance as in Carlisle as late as 1820 when it was [...] that friends of an anatomised man were so outraged that they took revenge on the doctors involved, and all who participated in the dissection were injured. One doctor was shot in the face and carried marks of his injury to the grave. Another participant was found dead after being thrown over the parapet of a high bridge. And if the dissection of criminals was looked upon with disfavour, despoliation of the graves of the innocent was considered something much worse.

Throughout the eighteenth century supply of corpses more or less kept pace with demand, so no great scandal arose. But the sudden increase in the study of anatomy at the beginning of the nineteenth century together with a passion for dissection created a chronic dearth of subjects. In Edinburgh the shortage became desperate due to the fantastic success of Barclay and Knox, and grave-robbing increased to such an extent that the city was in a state of near panic. Watch towers were built in churchyards, patrols were instituted by relatives of the dead, heavy iron mortsafes were placed over new graves, patent-locking coffins were offered for sale, and a host of other precautions were taken to foil the grave-robbers. Indeed, the ingenuity of the public was matched only by that of the resurrectionists!

The resurrectionists were skilled men, who worked carefully and expertly—they had to, because of the watches which were set and the traps which were laid for them. Spring guns were set up to catch them, and some were injured or even killed on body-snatching expeditions. Because of these traps a careful reconnaissance was usually made by day in the guise of mourners or workmen. Then at night the resurrectionists would return and dig away the earth to expose the head of the coffin. This task was not too difficult as the earth in a new grave was still loose, and could be removed quickly and easily. The soil was laid carefully on tarpaulin sheets so that there would be no marks left to betray the fact that the grave had been robbed. With the aid of a grappling iron the coffin lid was snapped off and a rope tied round the neck of the subject which was then dragged out of the coffin and up to the surface. Stealing a body was no crime in the eyes of the law, but taking a shroud was, so the body was immediately stripped of any clothing before it was put into a sack and taken away.

The sack-'em-up men could open a grave, remove a body and restore the soil between patrols of the night watch, and they could carry out the work so neatly that relatives of the subject could mourn by the grave the following day, unaware that their loved one was gracing some anatomy slab in Edinburgh.

Resurrectionists came in two classes—students of anatomy who wanted to augment the supply for their school, and professionals or semi-professionals who were in business to make money from the trade.

The students were enthusiastic amateurs to whom body-snatching was an adventure which added a dimension to their academic lives. There was great rivalry between students of the various schools, and sometimes a fight would take place to gain possession of a subject. Many of the most eminent surgeons of the first half of the nineteenth century were involved in body-snatching in their student days. Robert Liston was prominent among them, and once when he heard of the death of a child in Fife, who had suffered from hydrocephalus, he decided to get hold of the body. Relatives of the child knew that the resurrectionists were interested in the body, and for weeks the grave was guarded night and day. At last the daytime guard was relaxed and Liston and Ben Crouch, one of the most famous London resurrectionists, decided to snatch the body. Dressed as gentlemen travellers they arrived at an inn close to the graveyard, and there they left their dogcart with instructions that they were awaiting a parcel which a servant would deliver, but in the meantime they would stretch their legs. Soon a man appeared, dressed as a servant, and placed a large bag in the cart. Some time later the two men returned and were told that the parcel had been delivered. They drove off, but within a short time the night watch arrived at the grave and found it open and the body gone. By that time Liston and Crouch were well on their way to Edinburgh with their trophy.

The professional resurrectionists were the scum of society—criminals, prizefighters, ne'er-do-wells and sharp-witted, deft-handed men who did not care how they made money. They were experts—so expert that in the hour of gloaming before the night watch came on duty they could open a grave and remove the corpse.

Edinburgh had its share of professional resurrectionists, and their names—or rather nicknames, for they seldom used their real names in case any transaction might be traced back to them—were known and feared by the anatomists. Best known were 'Stupe', 'Spune', 'Merry Andrew' Merrilees and 'Moudiewarp' (the Mole). Of them all Merry Andrew was best known and cleverest. Alexander Leighton described him: "Of gigantic height, he was thin and gaunt, even to ridiculousness, with a long pale face, and the jaws of an ogre. His shabby clothes, no doubt made for some tall person of proportionate girth, hung upon his sharp joints more as if they had been placed there to dry than to clothe and keep him warm. Nor less grotesque were the motions and gestures of this strange being. It seemed as if he went upon springs and even the muscles of his face, as they passed from the grin of idiot pleasure to the scowl of anger, seemed to obey a similar power."

The doctors seldom asked questions of the resurrectionists with whom they dealt in case they might be frightened off and take their business to the rival school. They knew, too, that these men could be spiteful and vengeful to those who broke the strange code of honour under which they operated.

The resurrectionists drove a hard bargain. At the beginning of the new session they would swagger round the dissecting rooms bowing courteously to the lecturers and demonstrators, then they would ask what the lecturer was proposing to pay this year.

"Oh, I don't know, Murphy," the superintendent would reply, "whatever's fair. What will you take this morning?"

"Nothing, I thank you, Mr ——, but I don't mean to work this season without I get 10 guineas for a subject."

"Oh, indeed, well we don't mean to go more than 8."

"Then you may go and tell Sir —— that he may raise his own subjects for not one will he get from us."

A few weeks later Murphy would return and a bargain would be struck. The anatomists had to spend large sums of money supporting the families of resurrectionists who landed in jail and in return they often received little thanks. It was common enough for a gang to sell a body to a school and that night break in and steal it so that they could sell it to another anatomist. It was not unknown, too, for the sack or box to contain one of the gang very much alive, and ready to cut his way out at dead of night leaving the unsuspecting surgeon an old sack or an empty box.

When they were crossed or believed themselves to have been treated unfairly the resurrectionists were bitter opponents. They would leave bodies in the street close to the anatomy school so that a riot would be caused when it was discovered. At other times they mutilated a lecturer's subjects so that they would be of no value to him. Even among their own class they carried on this vicious warfare, and in cemeteries fights between rival gangs would terrorise a neighbourhood. Not surprisingly, the anatomists went out of their way to avoid offending their suppliers.

The bodysnatchers did not always have to open graves. They watched the crowded lodging houses of the city, listening to gossip about the sick and the dying, ready to move in before relatives or the undertaker as soon as death struck. Merry Andrew would present himself at the door of a lodging house and, looking suitably sad, claim to be a relative from the country.

He would tell a harrowing tale of the unfortunate man or woman, and say he would return later when he had arranged the burial. In due course he would reappear with a coffin and hearse, and occasionally a confederate known as 'Praying Howard', dressed as a minister, who would say a prayer over the coffin.

The resurrectionists did not trust even their closest collaborators. When Merry Andrew's sister died in Penicuik, Spune and Moudiewarp, who bore him a grudge at that moment, decided to exhume her body and sell it to the anatomists. They hired a horse and cart and drove to the graveyard where it was a simple matter to open the grave and remove the corpse. As they were about to leave a huge, wailing apparition dressed in white appeared from behind a tombstone, and Spune and Moudiewarp—hardened to visiting graveyards at night—took to their heels and fled, leaving the ghost in possession of the body. It was, of course, Merry Andrew himself, who had heard of the hiring of the cart and suspected what was afoot.

A little later Andrew came upon the two fugitives about to climb on to their cart, and he shouted "Stop thief!" which put them to flight. Andrew put his sister's body into the cart, and drove to Edinburgh, where the doctors were pleased to buy it.

The students, too, tried to outdo the professionals, and sometimes succeeded. One night a student passing along a street in the old town saw Merry Andrew waiting outside a house and, suspecting the reason, whispered as he walked past, "She's dead." Andrew hurried into the house and said in a loud voice to the nurse with whom he had a pact to buy the body, "It's a' owre then. When will we come for the corp'?"

"Wheesht, ye mongerel," hissed the nurse, "she's as lively as a cricket."

The patient heard it all and, not surprisingly, died in a state of terror the following night. Andrew and Spune returned to clinch the bargain, but the nurse was now very troubled. "A light has come down upon me frae heaven," she said, "I canna."

It took much time, money and drink to persuade the woman to change her mind, and in the midst of the negotiations a stranger arrived at the house. "Is Mrs Wilson dead?" he asked earnestly. "I am her nephew come to pay her the last tribute of affection."

The resurrectionists fled, with the nephew at their heels. They were not to know that it was the same student completing the prank which his whisper in the doorway had begun the night before.

For all their enthusiasm and ruses Merry Andrew and his friends, together with the students of Edinburgh, could not produce enough material to keep the anatomy schools stocked by the early part of the nineteenth century when dissection had become a passion among the doctors. More bodies were needed and it now became necessary to look to the south and to Ireland for material to augment the local supply. This pushed prices up alarmingly, and a subject which, in 1800, would have cost a guinea now was offered at 8 or 10 guineas.

Dublin, especially, became a useful source of supply and the

anatomy school of the Royal College of Surgeons there was suspected for many years of being used as a storeroom for bodies
waiting to be exported. The Irish capital was an easy source for
the further reason that many of the old graveyards were not
properly enclosed and could be entered without difficulty. The
free burial ground, Bully's Acre, was especially inviting since it
held the lowest and poorest about whom no one cared, and so the
resurrectionists had little to fear as they worked there.

A retired Scottish naval surgeon, called Wilson Rea, was
attracted to this easy source of money, and he built up so great an
export trade that he could not find enough bodies. He employed
sack-'em-up men to collect corpses and, with his wife who was
said to have superintended the shipment of them, he did very well.
Many of his subjects were smuggled into Britain, often through
the little deserted harbours on the Ayrshire coast where an enter-
prising general practitioner named Paterson organised much of the
business.

A large number of subjects were shipped openly in packing
cases labelled 'Pianos', 'Books', or very occasionally 'Animals for
museums'. From time to time a great scandal blew up when a
shipment was delayed, and the contents of the cases became
apparent from the odour emitted from them. The *Gentlemen's
Magazine* reported in October 1826, that a 'horrible discovery'
had been made aboard the ship *Latona* which was about to sail
from Liverpool to Leith. Three casks on board were found to
contain human bodies, some of them perfect, others mutilated,
and all in a most shocking state of decomposition. Police were sent
to the address from which the casks had been consigned and after
breaking down the doors of a cellar—"a place well calculated for
concealment"—they found another eleven casks, "all of which,
on being broken open, were found to contain human bodies in a
state too painful to describe: some were perfect, others dissected,
and some, we shudder at the recital, were put 'into pickle'. On
extending their search, seven sacks were discovered, containing
also the violated remains of the dead. The whole number of bodies
thus found to have been taken from the silent tomb was no less
than thirty-five."

On 10th July 1827, *The Times* carried a report that a box addressed to a Mr Thompson at 27 Percy Street, Bedford Square, London, had burst open at Liverpool revealing the body of an elderly man. The corpse bore no marks of violence and the doctor who was called in to examine it gave it as his opinion that it had been resurrected from a grave. The mate of the ship was brought before the coroner, but he claimed he had received the box from the shipping company's store in Dublin, so he was set free and orders were given to bury the body.

There was a similar scandal in Glasgow when a ship arrived with a cargo of what was purported to be cotton or linen rags, all neatly done up in sacks and addressed to a huckster in Jamaica Street. The consignee refused to pay £50 or £60 demanded for freight, so the cargo was sent back to the Broomielaw where it lay until the stench grew so strong that the city officers were called to open the sacks. Inside were found putrid bodies of men, women and children, and the authorities ordered them to be buried in Anderston churchyard. The explanation was simple: the subjects had come from Ireland, and were destined for anatomy lecturers in Edinburgh. Unfortunately the intermediary, the huckster, had not been warned to expect the cargo, otherwise he would no doubt have paid the freight dues and earned a large sum in commission.

Sometimes the bodies were sent by road, and at Carlisle inquests were often held on bodies which were discovered on the northbound coach. The verdict 'found dead in a box' was returned so often that it became a joke in the town.

If things were bad in Scotland at the beginning of the century, they were soon to become worse. Thrusting Liston arrived on the scene to spoil the pact which existed between Monro and Barclay, and soon the anatomists were at their wits' end to find enough subjects even with the imports from England and Ireland. And as rage against grave-robbing increased everywhere in the United Kingdom it rose to its greatest pitch in Scotland. Resurrectionists had always had to take extra care north of the border because religious feeling against despoiling the dead was greater there by far.

In 1813 a great storm arose in Glasgow over Granville Sharp

Pattison, one of the best known surgical lecturers in the city. Under Pattison's instruction a group of students, it was said, made raids on churchyards from time to time, but in 1813 two deaths aroused special interest among the medical fraternity in the city. The bodies were buried, one in Ramshorn Churchyard and the other in the Cathedral Churchyard, and the students at once set about raising both. At the Cathedral they were lucky and got not only the corpse they had come for but another as well, both of which were taken back to their rooms. Drink flowed so freely to celebrate this success that they made much noise when they went to Ramshorn Churchyard later and the alarm was raised. The students were chased and were seen to disappear in the direction of the University.

Next day the search was resumed not only by the police but by a crowd seeking vengeance. So great was the furore that every suspected person's house was searched and parts of a body, believed to be a Mrs McAlister, were found. Pattison and his assistants were arrested, and the lecturer was put on trial. Although the defence succeeded in proving that the body was not Mrs McAlister, and Pattison was acquitted, he had to leave Glasgow and emigrate to America where he became an eminent surgeon.

With so many scandals and outrages it is not surprising that the strictest precautions were taken to guard the newly buried. The *Gentlemen's Magazine* warned in the autumn of 1826 that the time was now near when it might reasonably be expected that stealing of bodies would begin. "I understand," their correspondent wrote, "that in Glasgow graves have been watched by people furnished with firearms." Indeed they were. In the graveyard at Carmunnock the regulations for watchers, drawn up in 1828, read: "There are two on watch each night, who are to go on after sunset, and continue till after daybreak in winter, and till after sunrise in summer. They are strictly forbidden from getting intoxicated, or leaving the churchyard during that time; no visitor is allowed to enter on any account without the password for the night. They are also prohibited from making any noise or firing guns, except when giving alarm, that any of the inhabitants in such case may turn out to the assistance of the watch."

Despite all these precautions the *Gentlemen's Magazine* correspondent who had issued the warning quoted one anatomy school as reporting "an ample supply of bodies as usual". He could have been quoting Dr Robert Knox of Surgeons' Square in Edinburgh.

Such was the state of the market when Knox was at the height of his fame. He needed more subjects than any other anatomist because he had more students. In a single year he spent £700 on subjects for his anatomy classes—and at £8 to £10 each, which was then the standard purchasing price—this represented something like eighty corpses. He bought all he could in Edinburgh, but he also had to send to London and Dublin to satisfy the demand his success created.

Knox boasted that he could always obtain bodies, but the price he paid was sometimes high. On one occasion he paid 25 guineas for a body rather than disappoint a class, but Knox was to pay more yet. The price he finally paid was his career.

TWO

Fiends Meet

In Edinburgh during the 1820s the stolid Scottish community was leavened by large numbers of Irish immigrants who found poverty in Scotland preferable to starvation at home. They moved from one town to another and from city to country as work or rumours of work called them. These Irishmen were a wild community who drank even harder than their Scottish neighbours, and who kept together more clannishly than any Scots. Among them were William Burke and William Hare who were to become notorious as the West Port murderers.

Burke was born at a place called Orrey in County Tyrone in 1792, the son of a respectable couple who were hard put to scratch an existence from the land. He and his brother Constantine had a better education than most other children in these parts, and when they grew up they escaped from the poverty around them by joining the army. While serving with the Donegal Militia William met and married a girl from Ballina in County Mayo, and at the end of his service he went to live there. Rumour said that he had seven children of whom only one lived, but that seems impossible for he could not have been married very long when he fell out with his father-in-law in about 1818 over a lease of some land and walked out on his family. It is much more probable that he deserted his wife and two children, as he claimed in one of his confessions, because they would not come with him to Scotland.

He moved to Scotland where labourers were wanted to help on the works of the Union Canal. The diggings had reached the Polmont area, so he settled in the village of Maddiston, and it was there that he met Helen McDougal, the only Scot among the four leading characters in the West Port Murders case. At that time she was living with a sawyer named McDougal whose name she had taken, not through marriage, for she had deserted her legal husband to live with McDougal, but for convenience or for the sake of the two children she had borne McDougal.

One wonders what William, a man "of a very social and agreeable disposition with a great turn for raillery and jocularity", saw in this large-boned Scottish woman whose dour, ill-proportioned face mirrored her stolid disagreeable nature. Whatever the attraction, William and Nelly lived together—not very faithfully—as husband and wife until murder and its consequences parted them. Nelly was very jealous, and this trait led to many quarrels for William was constantly unfaithful.

When the canal works were finished Burke and Nelly drifted into Edinburgh and just managed to earn a living by peddling old clothes round the doors and by going round the surrounding countryside collecting skins and human hair to sell in the city. William learnt to mend shoes, and was soon earning upwards of a pound a week by collecting old shoes, repairing them, and selling them round the doors. One major disaster befell them at this time when they lost everything in a fire at Micky Culzean's lodging house in the West Port.

In Edinburgh in those early days Burke was known as an industrious, happy man, greatly given to music and singing. He would persuade an Italian boy who played a barrel organ in the streets to provide music for an impromptu dance or concert. Although nominally a Roman Catholic, he preferred to attend prayer meetings in the Grassmarket, and was regarded as one of the most regular and intelligent members of the congregation. On Sundays he was seldom seen without a Bible in his hand.

So William and Nelly drifted in and out of the town, working on farms during the summer and autumn and in the city in winter. For a while they lived in Peebles, where their house was known for miles around as a gathering place for low and drunken Irishmen every Saturday and Sunday. Burke left Peebles to go harvesting, owing his landlady more than two pounds, and promised to repay the debt. Needless to say he never did, and when the rumours of the West Port murders began to circulate the landlady told how she had written to him asking for repayment and had been asked to meet him at a lonely spot on the Edinburgh road at ten o'clock one night. And she knew what would have happened if she had kept that appointment!

During this time Burke fell in with a countryman, William Hare, who had been rather more fortunate. His new friend was born at Newry, and had also worked on the Union Canal, but they do not seem to have known one another at the time. While working on the canal Hare met a man called Logue who organised a gang of Irish labourers, and who kept a tramps' lodging house in a filthy, wretched alley off the West Port called Tanner's Close because it led to a tannery at the rear of the 'land'.

Logue's house was a low, two-storeyed building standing on sloping ground at the back of a tall old town 'land', and it was approached through a close and down a few steps. It looked conventional enough, with windows flanking the front door and three small-paned windows on the upper storey. A flight of five or six broken steps led to the waste land where the tannery stood. Outside hung a sign, "BEDS TO LET".

Logue had the lower part of the house which consisted of three rooms. The one just inside the door was largest, and it had been cleared of furniture and filled with beds all round its walls. A second large room opened off it, and this was furnished in exactly the same way. The third apartment was no more than a large cupboard with a small window looking out on to a pigsty and a dead wall.

It was a filthy place and the only comfort its inhabitants had was drink. There was constant coming and going of people, and brawling was commonplace, so it is not surprising that cries of murder went unheard or unheeded. As the guests slept two or three to a bed the lodging house brought a tidy sum to Logue at a charge of threepence a person each night.

When the canal was completed and Hare found work loading and unloading the canal boats, he moved into his friend Logue's house. Logue's new lodger was a repulsive looking character, who

32

WILLIAM BURKE.
THE MURDERER

WILLIAM HARE.
KING'S EVIDENCE

appeared at first sight to be a simpleton. The first thing one noticed was his dull, dead, blackish reptilian eyes, set wide apart, and one rather higher than the other. He had a large coarse-lipped mouth and high, broad cheek bones. When he laughed, which was often, his sunken cheeks collapsed into perpendicular hollows which shot up ghastlily from chin to cheekbone.

For a time all was well at Tanner's Close, but Hare and his landlord fell out—probably because Hare was making romantic overtures to Mrs Logue—and Hare was shown the door. However, news travelled fast in the crowded old town of Edinburgh, and when Hare heard one day in 1826 that Logue had died, he returned to the lodging house to console the widow. Mrs Logue was already being comforted by another lodger, but Hare soon had the rival turned out and took over the widow and the house.

As in the case of Burke and Nelly McDougal it was not beauty that attracted Hare to Mrs Logue, although she was a somewhat less dour person. She was hard-featured, tight-lipped, tough, and far from attractive. She had worked alongside her husband on the canal diggings, dressed in a navvy's jacket and wheeling a barrow as well as any man. She was continually debauched, and her nickname of 'Lucky' seemed singularly inappropriate. There can be no doubt that it was her lodging house and not her face that was her fortune.

William and Lucky never went through a marriage ceremony and in the eyes of the Church—they were both Roman Catholics—they were living in sin, but under the law of Scotland they were married by reason of having lived together as husband and wife.

Unlike Burke, Hare was considered a perfect pest around the West Port. He and Lucky fought frequently in the streets and at home, and both were known to be hard and capable of the vilest crime. Indeed, it was rumoured that they murdered a child Lucky bore him early in their acquaintance, and buried the body in a box on the waste ground at the bottom of Tanner's Close. Burke and Hare soon became firm friends; so close that when they were harvesting together on the farm of Carlinden near Carnwath and Hare received a letter to say that his child was ill, Nelly remarked,

33

"If Hare goes, William Burke will go too, for they are like brothers." All four then left together.

The Burkes returned from harvesting at Penicuik at the end of the autumn of 1827, and settled into their winter routine of shoe-mending and peddling their wares round the doors of Edinburgh. They had now moved into Tanner's Close, and drank regularly and excessively with their landlord and landlady. They had as a fellow lodger an old army pensioner called Donald, who was in poor health. As the autumn advanced Donald's health failed and Hare took on a worried look. Hare was not really concerned about whether Donald lived or died for there were plenty of others who would be glad of his bed: he did not want the old man to die at that moment because he owed Hare £4 and could not repay it until his pension became due in a few weeks' time. Hare watched, hoped, and willed the old man to live, but Donald steadily became more feeble and on 29th November he died.

Hare was in despair, and took his problem to his friend Burke. After long and earnest discussion Hare himself suggested a solution. They were familiar with low life in Edinburgh and probably knew some of the resurrection men although they had never taken part in the trade. Why not pretend that they had stolen Donald's body from its grave, said Hare, and sell it to Professor Monro at the University. Burke thought this would be an excellent plan and, although he had no idea of the procedure for disposing of a corpse to the anatomists, he readily agreed to help.

It was well known to neighbours and to the other lodgers that Donald had died, so it was essential for the body to appear to be buried. The undertaker was called in and he put Donald into a coffin and arranged for the funeral to take place at Greyfriars churchyard. While this was being organised the two slipped out to the tannery at the back of the house and collected a sack of tanner's bark. Hare prised off the coffin lid with a chisel, and they removed the body and filled the coffin with bark. The lid was replaced, and the two looked duly mournful when the undertaker returned.

As soon as they thought it safe they set out for the University to try to contact Professor Monro, but they were new to the resurrec-

34

tion business and did not realise that most of the transactions were done at night. At the University they asked for directions from a student who happened to belong to the rival school of Dr Knox, and he advised them to try No 10 Surgeons' Square. The young man could not have realised that he had taken the first step towards ruining his master's career.

At Dr Knox's rooms Burke and Hare had no idea how to open negotiations, and they and the doctor's assistants talked round the purpose of the visit for a long time before Burke and Hare came to the point of admitting that they had a body for sale. Burke and Hare were agreeably surprised to learn that the doctor might be prepared to pay as much as £10 for a suitable corpse, and they went away with instructions to bring the body round after dark. The practice in anatomy schools was for the lecturer's senior assistants to be on duty each night on a rota system to receive subjects brought in by resurrectionists, and to pay for them.

On duty that night when Burke and Hare arrived were David Paterson, the doorkeeper, whose job was to record the dates of visits and names of the men who brought subjects, and three assistants, William Fergusson, Thomas Wharton Jones and Alexander Miller, all of whom were later to become famous surgeons. Burke and Hare gave their names simply as John and William, and they were asked to carry their sack up to the lecture room where the assistants waited.

There the two were ordered to remove the body from the sack, and take off the shroud, so that the doctor's men might examine the subject. Donald's body was then laid on the dissecting table and thoroughly examined, but no questions were asked about the freshness of the body or the fact that it had never been buried, although this must have been seemed unusual to Fergusson and his colleagues. However, the policy of the anatomists was to ask as few questions as possible in case the resurrectionists were frightened off and took their custom elsewhere.

The assistants were well pleased with the subject, but they offered only £7 10s instead of the standard £10. Perhaps they realised that the two Irishmen were newcomers to the resurrection trade, and so they decided to make a better bargain for their

35

master. Burke and Hare were delighted. They had never handled such a sum of money before, and gladly accepted the offer. As they disappeared into the darkness of Surgeons' Square a voice called after them, "Good night, gentlemen, we shall be glad to see you again when you have any other bodies to dispose of."

In the dark, silent square they counted out the money. Hare kept £4 5s, which covered his debt comfortably, and handed over £3 5s to Burke, which seems more than generous considering how minor a role Burke claims to have played in the whole business. Indeed it makes one suspect that Burke was more deeply involved in the matter than he admitted. For the moment both were content, for they had as much money in their pockets as they might earn in a whole month, and it had not required hard work to come by it.

They deserved a drink, and for once they had plenty of money to pay for it.

THREE

The Ladies Vanish

The two Williams were well satisfied with their deal over Donald's body. They had enough money in their pockets to keep work at bay for a considerable time, and provide drink to relieve the squalid life of Tanner's Close. However, even such a large sum could not last for ever, and Burke had to return to his trade of repairing shoes and selling them round the doors. Hare was working on the loading and unloading of boats on the Union Canal.

It is perfectly possible that Burke and Hare might have regarded Donald's death as a fortunate chance never to be repeated, and they might not have thought of selling another body to the doctors had temptation not presented itself at Tanner's Close. Another of Hare's lodgers, a miller named Joseph, was taken ill suddenly, and within a day or two ran a high fever and became delirious.

As Joseph's condition worsened, Hare and his wife grew more solemn—this could be cholera or typhoid, or any of a dozen other infections which broke out the crowded, insanitary old town from time to time and spread death mercilessly from house to house. Nothing could be worse for business in the lodging house if word of Joseph's illness got around.

It was natural for Hare to turn once again to his friend, and ask him to come and look at the sick man. Joseph was bound to die, they decided, so why not ease his end and offer his body to the doctor. After all, the assistants at No 10 Surgeons' Square had said they would be glad to see them again when they had another body to sell.

When Joseph recovered consciousness for a moment they

produced the whisky bottle and put it to his lips. The miller was weak, but he drank gratefully, then slipped into a coma once more. At a signal Burke took a pillow and placed it over Joseph's nose and mouth, while Hare threw himself across the body in case of resistance. But the fever and whisky had done their work well: Joseph was too weak to fight.

This time they did not take the trouble to obtain a coffin and arrange a mock funeral. They simply put the body into a sack and hid it until dead of night when they crept through the empty streets to Surgeons' Square. At Dr Knox's lecture rooms they were welcomed by the assistants who remembered them. The body was laid out on the dissecting table in the usual manner and examined. Clearly it was considered a better buy than the previous one, for the doctors offered £10 this time. Again no questions were asked and no information was offered by 'John' and 'William'.

Christmas came and went, and so did the £10. But fortune did not desert Tanner's Close. Edinburgh was full of beggars, itinerant packmen and prostitutes who had neither permanent homes nor relatives who would report their disappearance. A large element of the population shifted between city and country and between Edinburgh and other towns as the mood took them or as rumours of work beckoned. In these surroundings the disappearance of a character from the streets would not be talked about for more than a day, and the last thing any acquaintances were likely to do was go to the police. If subjects would not come to Tanner's Close, then Burke and Hare would go out and find them.

In the brief, freezing days of early February 1828, the two men moved through the old town watching and waiting for a suitable victim. Often they were unlucky and their victim would escape, or there would be too many lodgers in Tanner's Close for them to be able to carry out the murder. However, one day they found Abigail Simpson.

Abigail was old, she was poor, and she had few friends. She had once worked for Sir John Hope, and in her old age he allowed her a pension of eighteenpence and a can of broth, which she eked out by selling salt and camstone. She was glad to walk to Edinburgh from her home at Gilmerton to collect her allowance each week.

38

On 11th February Abigail slipped her blue spotted shawl over her shoulders and set out to collect her pension as usual. When she had the eighteenpence in her purse and her can of broth in her hand she did not go straight home, but dallied in the city, probably to sell salt round the doors or just to drink at one of the taverns. Burke claimed that she met the Hares who invited her to Tanner's Close, but when Burke made his allegation he was anxious to implicate Hare in the murders as deeply as he could. It is possible that Burke knew Abigail and lured her to Tanner's Close himself, for at the time of the murders a story was told of how Burke once made fun of a female salt vendor whom he heard yelling discordantly, "Wha'll buy saut?"

Affecting an overpolite manner he turned to the woman and said, "Upon my word I do not know, but if you will ask that woman standing gaping at the door opposite, she will perhaps be able to inform you."

It does not matter whether it was Burke or Hare who lured Abigail to the lodging house: what is important is that she went. At Tanner's Close the bottle was passed round again and again, so that the guest and her hosts all became merry. February days are short and Gilmerton was a long, cold walk away, so Hare suggested that Abigail should stay the night with them. When Abigail's eighteenpence had all been spent on drink, Margaret Hare bought her can of soup for another one shilling and sixpence, which was duly spent on whisky.

Hare had become very jolly and when Abigail told him she had a daughter he said that he was a single man and would marry her to get all the money amongst them. The party continued long into the evening at such a pace that when the moment came for Burke and Hare to implement their plan they were as incapable as their victim.

In the morning Abigail was a sorry sight: she felt sick and was suffering badly from her evening's drinking. Hare recommended more whisky and Abigail drank that and some beer as well. Soon she was as drunk as she had been the previous evening, and lay down on a bed where she fell asleep. Burke and Hare had taken care to remain sober and they now crept over to her bed. At a signal Burke seized Abigail's hands and feet while Hare covered her nose and mouth. The poor woman hardly stirred, and within a few minutes she was dead.

They undressed the body, put it into a tea chest, and hurried off to tell the doctors that they had another subject ready for them. That night Burke and Hare carried the box to a dark rendezvous at the foot of the Castle Rock, and there they met a porter whom Alexander Miller had sent to meet them. The murderers followed the porter to No 10 Surgeons' Square where, for the first time, they met the great anatomist, Robert Knox.

The doctor examined the body himself, and commented on how fresh it was. However, he did not probe the reasons for this freshness, and willingly authorised payment of £10.

Burke and Hare took their leave. They were a month's earnings better off: Dr Knox had gained a fine subject: Edinburgh had lost a character, but never missed her. So far as is known no one fretted over the disappearance of the old salt vendor, Abigail Simpson.

The £10 which Dr Knox paid for Abigail's body was divided out. The first £1 went to Margaret Hare who insisted, as owner of the lodging house which was such a convenient centre of operations, on this share every time. Hare then received £5 and Burke £4.

It was impossible to conceal so much money and all four began to dress better and to drink more. This elevation of their standard of living was noticed and talked about in so small a community as the West Port, so the four put about a story of a legacy which they had inherited. Occasionally Nelly would say that money was running short and their clothes would go into pawn, so she would say that she had written off for more money, and a few days later she would be in funds again. Burke would hint darkly that he was a resurrectionist or at other times that he smuggled a little illicit whisky. Nelly was never short of a tale to explain away their affluence. In addition to the legacy story she said she had property in Stirlingshire which her former husband had left to her, and once she even said that William was the favourite of a lady in the New Town who never allowed him to go short of money.

When Nelly said that they had sent off for another part of the legacy it was a sign that another murder was due. Unfortunately those to whom she made the remark did not appreciate its full meaning. If only they had . . .

An Englishman who sold matches round the streets of the city now came to lodge with the Hares, and after quite a short time he became ill. Soon his skin took on the yellow tinge which could only mean jaundice. The Hares dreaded the effect this would have on their business, but this time they did not have to search for a solution.

Hare threw himself on top of the sick man so that he could not move, while Burke suffocated him by putting his hands to the Englishman's nose and mouth. They did not realise it, but by chance they had stumbled on a method which left no marks, and which made it almost impossible to detect that the victim had met a violent death.

They did not know this old man's name or where he came from, so they could not have answered questions even if any had been asked—which they were not. Within a few hours the matchseller was laid out on Dr Knox's marble slab and pronounced suitable for dissection.

Neither Burke nor Hare knew the name of the next victim, who was an old woman enticed into Tanner's Close by Mrs Hare and plied with whisky. She must have had a better head for alcohol than most of their victims because Lucky made three attempts to force the old woman to lie down before she finally did so and fell asleep in a stupor. William Hare found the victim awaiting him when he returned from the canal wharf to have his dinner. He calmly folded part of the bed-tick over her mouth and nose and went off and ate his meal. When he returned in the evening he checked and found that the woman was dead.

Burke had no hand in this murder, but that night he helped to dispose of the body to Dr Knox for another £10.

The next murder is important because more details are known of it than of most others. The victim was Mary Paterson. Mary and her friend Janet were in their late teens, yet both were experienced prostitutes, well known in the streets of Edinburgh. Mary was extremely beautiful, but beauty did little to mitigate the pain of being poor in Edinburgh in 1828. Her parents had died when she was still young, and it was while scraping an existence in the streets of the city that she fell in with bad company and took to prostitution. At least that brought some money even if it did mean a constant battle of wits with the law.

On the night of Tuesday, 8th April, Mary and Janet were caught by the police and kept in the Canongate police office overnight. At six in the morning they were released, and went to the house of a Mrs Lawrie with whom they had once lodged. They were well received by Mrs Lawrie, who seems to have been a mother figure to the girls, but as soon as the city came to life they went out in search of drink.

In William Swanston's shop in the Canongate they shared a gill of whisky and, as they drank, they were aware of a stranger who watched them while he stood at the counter drinking rum and bitters with the proprietor. Soon the dark-eyed man drifted away from Swanston and joined the girls. Although William Burke was not known to Mary and Janet it is more than likely that he had seen them around the streets and knew them by sight. He bought them each a gill of rum and bitters, and when they had finished the drink, invited them to his house for breakfast. Mary was willing to go, but it took a considerable amount of his soft Irish talk to win Janet round.

Mary was not taken in by his boasts of the pension which he enjoyed, or by offers that he "could keep her handsomely and make her comfortable for life", but it was evident that he had enough money in his pocket to buy a bit of happiness for a street girl at that moment.

Mary and Janet at last agreed to go to Burke's lodgings, and as an indication of pleasures to come, he bought a bottle of whisky for each of them.

Burke led the girls to Gibb's Close off the Canongate, up a wooden stair, and along a dark passage to the house where his brother Constantine lived. Constantine and his wife were still in bed, and Burke, keeping up the pretence of being a lodger, cursed them and ordered them to get breakfast for him and his guests.

Constantine did not protest, but rose and kindled the fire, and Mrs Burke cooked a large breakfast of finnan haddocks, eggs, bread and tea, while the 'guests' passed the time drinking whisky. By the time breakfast was over the bottles were well on the way to being emptied.

Mary was tired and tipsy, and fell asleep where she sat at the table, but Janet had a stronger head and remained sober. When Burke suggested to Janet that they should go out for a stroll and leave Mary to sleep it off, the girl agreed. They did not get far though: within a few minutes they were in a tavern drinking beer and eating pies. Janet remained sober, however, until they returned to the house where Mary slept.

Burke was at his most charming, and the girl no doubt responded —after all that was her stock in trade—but the happy little scene was shattered as he fluttered round her and chaffed her with his Irish talk. The curtains which hid the bed suddenly parted, to reveal Nelly, looking as black as a January storm and quite as full of pent-up fury. William's blarney was too much for her dour Scottish soul, and she exploded into a tirade against Janet for seducing her husband, and against William for being faithless. Mrs Constantine, who materialised from some corner of the room, whispered somewhat unnecessarily to Janet that this was the gentleman's wife, and the girl explained that she had not been aware that he was married. Nelly now turned her full fury on her husband, and abused him so mercilessly that he lost his temper and threw a glass at her, gashing her forehead just above one eye. Burke pushed his bleeding wife out the door and locked it. He then tried to persuade Janet to lie down with him on the bed, but the girl was too frightened of the woman hammering on the door to agree. She begged to be allowed to go, and Burke finally escorted her past his angry wife and down the stair, but only after she had promised to return when Nelly was not around.

Constantine's wife had gone to fetch Hare, who came and found Mary Paterson still asleep. Within minutes the two men had murdered her, laid her body out on the bed, and hid it with a sheet.

In the meantime Janet returned to Mrs Lawrie's house and told her of the adventure, which she obviously regarded (in retrospect) as highly amusing, for she added, "We have got some fine lodgings now". Mrs Lawrie was not amused. She sent Janet straight back, accompanied by a servant girl, to bring Mary home, but in her confusion Janet could not find the house and had to go to Swanston's tavern to ask the way. She was given directions to Gibb's Close, but even then she went to the wrong door, and was sent upstairs to Burke's house by the inhabitants, who told her in no uncertain terms what they thought of their neighbours.

In Constantine's house she found the Hares and Nelly: Burke had gone out, probably to fetch drink. Margaret Hare made to attack the girl, but her husband restrained her, and explained that Mary had gone out with Burke and would soon be back. Janet sat down to wait, and was offered another drink which she accepted. She sent the maid home but Mrs Lawrie, now really alarmed, ordered the girl to go straight back with instructions to fetch Janet.

At last Mrs Lawrie's alarm communicated itself to Janet, who now obeyed, but promised to return later in the day. Janet did return, but this time she found only Constantine's wife in the house. Burke and Mary still had not come back, she was told, and of course she was not to know that at that moment Burke and Hare were trudging up the High School Yards, carrying a sack and pursued by a group of school boys who chanted, "They're carrying a corpse!" It was a nasty moment for the murderers, but their luck held and no policeman appeared to look into the sack. They were never so thankful to reach Surgeons' Square.

Mary Paterson's body was still warm when they reached Surgeons' Square, and for the first time Burke and Hare were asked questions. William Fergusson and a student, whom Burke described as "a tall lad", were on duty at the lecture rooms, and the student said Mary was as like a girl he had seen in the Canongate a few nights before "as one pea is like another". Fergusson asked Burke and Hare where they had got the body, and they replied that they had bought it from an old woman at the back of the Canongate. They asked Burke to cut off her hair, and gave him a pair of scissors to do the job. When that had been done they paid £8 for the body.

David Paterson, the doorkeeper, came into the room in the

middle of this discussion, and found Alexander Miller in conversation with Burke and Hare, standing beside a female subject stretched out on the floor. "The beautiful symmetry and freshness of the body attracted my attention," said Paterson later. "Soon after I heard Mr Fergusson, another assistant of Dr Knox, say that he was acquainted with the deceased, and named her as Mary Mitchell."

Paterson's curiosity was aroused, and the next time Burke and Hare visited No 10 Surgeons' Square Paterson asked where they had procured the body, and he was told that they had bought it from friends of the deceased.

Henry Lonsdale, who was one of Knox's students, wrote in his biography of the anatomist,

> The body of the girl Paterson could not fail to attract attention by its voluptuous form and beauty; students crowded around the table on which she lay, and artists came to study a model worthy of Phidias and the best Greek art; here was publicity beyond the professional walk; nay, more, a pupil of Knox's who had been in her company only a few nights previously, stood aghast on observing the beautiful Lais stretched in death, and ready for the scalpel of the anatomist. This student eagerly and sympathisingly sought for an explanation of her sudden death; Burke on his next visit was confronted with this questioner in the presence of two gentlemen, and declared that he bought the corpse from an old hag in the Canongate, and that Paterson had killed herself with drink. He offered to go and show the house if they doubted him. His explanation was feasible; it rested on the whisky tendency of all such women— and Paterson's body smelt of liquor when brought in—their reckless life and exposure, and their frequent abandonment when at death's door.

Mary's body was not dissected immediately. It was carefully preserved in whisky for three months so that Dr Knox could use her beautiful form to illustrate his lectures on muscular development. By that time she had been forgotten by everyone in Edinburgh, except perhaps the student who had lain close to her so short a time before she died, and Janet Brown, who continued to ask wherever she went if anyone had seen her friend.

FOUR

Friends for Sale

Old Effie spent her days gleaning among the ashpits in search of anything that might be exchanged for money to buy drink which would bring temporary oblivion. It was an endless process, for as soon as she was sober again she found herself as poor and miserable as ever and she had to resume the search among the cinders.

Effie had regular purchasers for the various types of flotsam which she discovered. Mr Burke, for example, would take scraps of leather to use for his shoe-mending. She knew Burke well, and was not suspicious when he asked her to go into the stable at Tanner's Close under some pretext, and offered her a drink while she was there. One dram led to another until Effie became first merry and then unconscious. Burke slipped out and fetched his confederate who helped Effie to pass on into permanent oblivion.

With each success Burke's boldness increased. One morning he met two policemen dragging a drunk woman to the West Port police office. Burke was in good spirits, and said to Andrew Williamson, one of the officers who happened to be his neighbour: "And what's this ould body been up to, Andrew?"

"Drunk," said the policeman sniffily. "We found her sitting on a stair drunk and incapable."

"Let her go to her lodgings then, and save yourselves a lot of trouble," Burke advised.

"But we don't know where she bides, Mr Burke."

"It's all right, I know her house well. I'll take her there for you."

Williamson and his colleague were glad to be rid of the old

woman, and handed her over willingly. Burke took her arm and humped her along the West Port, while the policemen returned thankfully to their duties. No one noticed Burke lead the woman into Tanner's Close, and no one saw her leave it, for her body was carried out by the back way at dead of night and taken to Surgeons' Square where Dr Knox's assistants were pleased to pay £10 for it as a subject for dissection.

Burke was highly skilled in the art of picking victims off the street. In the early part of June 1828, he came upon a poor old man in the High Street, and at once set about coaxing him into the trap. Coaxing is an exaggeration, for the man was already as near to drunkenness as his money would take him, and he readily agreed to go and share a dram with Burke. However, on the way to Tanner's Close the two men were stopped by an old Irish-woman who led a boy of about 12 years of age by the hand. The woman told her tale: she and her deaf mute grandson had walked all the way from Glasgow to Edinburgh in search of some friends, but now they could not find the house. Burke at once abandoned the old man (probably thinking that he could come back later and find him again) and turned his attention to the woman. The old man did not know what a narrow escape he had had, and was furious at losing the promised drink. Burke ignored his protests and devoted himself to the woman and her grandson. Of course he knew where their friends lived, and he would take them there, but it was a good step and they had better come to his house for a bite to eat first. At Tanner's Close the old woman was plied with drink in the usual manner until she fell asleep in the little back room. Then, while Nelly and Lucky looked after the boy in the main room of the lodging house, Burke and Hare suffocated her.

What was to be done with the boy? The four talked the matter over and at first they thought of taking him into the maze of streets and courts that made up the old town and losing him. But there were risks attached to that: he might find his way back to Tanner's Close and make someone understand that his grandmother had vanished there. It was decided, therefore, that the boy must die.

Still they hesitated. Nothing was done that night, or even the following morning when Hare went out to get a box to hold the bodies. Several versions of the boy's death are given. In Burke's confessions he was said to have been smothered and laid on the bed beside his grandmother, but it is generally believed that the boy became anxious about the disappearance of his grandmother and was restless and whimpered. Burke took the boy on to his knee, and without warning broke his back.

The bodies were crammed into an old herring barrel and loaded on to the cart which Hare was using for his current business enterprise of hawking fish and crockery round the doors. His old horse was hitched up and they set off along the Cowgate. Like most other things connected with William Hare, the horse was decrepit and useless: it had two large sores on its shoulder which had been stuffed with cotton and covered with a piece of horse's skin to prevent discovery, and the beast was barely able to put one foot past the other. At the Mealmarket it gave up altogether, and all the cajoling and cursing that Burke and Hare could muster had no effect. When a crowd began to gather one of them hurried off to find a porter who would carry the barrel the rest of the way.

At No 10 Surgeons' Square the students had great difficulty in removing the tightly-packed bodies from the barrel. Both were examined, pronounced satisfactory, and paid for at the standard summer rate of £8 each.

For the first time Burke was troubled by the terrible crime which he had committed. He was haunted by the recollection of the wistful, innocent eyes of the boy as they looked into his face that day when he was murdered. Burke would lie awake, haunted by the young face. Now he kept a bottle of whisky and a lighted candle at his bedside, and when the nightmare came he would take a long draught from the bottle—sometimes as much as half a bottle at a time—to lay the ghost.

What Burke needed was a change of scene, and the time for this was opportune because the ghoulish friendship was fraying at the edges. Nelly and Lucky were not getting on well together for a number of reasons, but especially because Lucky resented Nelly as an outsider—a dour, long-faced Scottish Presbyterian among three Irish Roman Catholics. She was also bitter about the fact that they were making free with what was, after all, her house, and

(*left*) Helen McDougal,
Burke's mistress

(*right*) 'Lucky' Hare
and her child

Dr Robert Knox lecturing in his fiftieth year

it must have been apparent to her that Burke was the brain behind the operation while her own stupid husband was incapable of organising such a lucrative business on his own.

There was a story current at the time that Lucky whispered to Burke that he should get rid of Nelly, and that he agreed to go away for a holiday, during which he would murder her and send back word to Tanner's Close that she had died. In view of his attachment to Nelly this seems highly unlikely. On the contrary, the choice of Nelly's home in Stirlingshire for the holiday in June 1828 indicates that the idea of the interlude from murder came from Nelly. After all she shared his bed and the haunting of his mind by the deaf-mute boy whom he had murdered so cruelly.

At midsummer they went away and stayed with Nelly's relatives for several weeks. The holiday did not heal the breach at Tanner's Close, however. On the contrary, on his return Burke suspected that Hare had been at work on his own and had not shared out the proceeds. Of course Hare denied this, but a few questions at Surgeons' Square revealed that Hare had in fact sold the body of a woman for £8. Burke was furious, and there followed a tremendous quarrel which resulted in Burke and Nelly marching out of the lodging house and moving in with John Brogan, who was married to Burke's cousin. Although the Brogans lived only two closes away from Tanner's Close, William and Nelly had nothing to do with the Hares for some weeks until they found that separation killed their trade. Together, Burke and Hare were a formidable force: apart they could do little.

In the close community of Edinburgh they could not fail to meet from time to time and, as tempers cooled, they drifted together again to resume their business. They did not have far to look for a victim.

A frequent visitor to the house at this time was Mrs Ostler, the widow of a porter, who lived in the Grassmarket and made a living by taking in washing. Mrs Ostler came to the 'land' because Mrs Lawrie, one of Burke's closest neighbours, had a mangle, and was willing to let her have the use of it. Doors stood open much of the time and Mrs Ostler visited the other houses when she called to do her mangling. She sometimes helped Mrs Brogan who was on the point of childbirth, and when the baby was born she joined in the celebrations. It was during this party that she was seen going into the house with Burke, singing "Sweet Home", and that was the last time she was seen.

The Brogans were as rough as their kinsmen and had a reputation of being rude, brutal and constantly brawling. There were many who believed that Brogan was involved in the murders too. Brogan was hopelessly in arrears with his rent, and Burke and Hare each gave him £1 10s to clear this, but instead Brogan disappeared with the money. That is how Burke came to take over the tenancy of the house and its furnishings.

The next victim was Ann McDougal, a cousin of Nelly's husband whom they had met in Stirlingshire and who had been invited to visit them in Edinburgh. The girl was enjoying the high life in Edinburgh after the country, so she was easily plied with whisky until she fell into a drunken sleep. When the moment came to murder her, Burke hesitated and told Hare to play the major role because the girl was "a distant friend" of his. Hare, therefore, put his hands on the girl's nose and mouth and suffocated her while Burke held her down.

Dr Knox's doorkeeper David Paterson provided "a fine trunk" into which the body was placed for transportation to Surgeons' Square after nightfall. There Ann McDougal's body raised £10.

It was impossible to continue to find enough subjects within the household, so Burke and Hare soon resumed their search of the streets: perhaps they had never given it up, but had just gone through a period when victims were easier to find at home.

One day Hare noticed an elderly prostitute, Mary Haldane, whom he knew, standing at the mouth of one of the closes which led off the Grassmarket. Mary had stayed at Tanner's Close in the past, and she gladly accepted his invitation to accompany him to the lodging house for a dram. She was a noted character around Edinburgh, doubly conspicuous because her smile revealed a single tooth which stood as large as a fencepost in the front of her mouth. Mary was fat, old and a figure of fun, tormented by children wherever she went. That morning was no exception and

Burke, who had a habit of materialising whenever there was business in the offing, drove her tormentors off and accompanied Mary and Hare to Tanner's Close.

The women, who were waiting at the lodging house, helped to entertain Mary until she was fit only to sleep. She went to the stable and fell asleep, and among the straw there she was murdered.

Mary was unmarried, but she had three daughters, one respectably married, one serving a sentence of fourteen years' transportation, and a third who followed in her mother's footsteps as a whore in Edinburgh. This last daughter, Peggy, missed her mother and soon began to search for her. She called at Rymer's shop in the West Port and was told that he mother had been seen going into Tanner's Close with Hare.

Peggy called at the house where her knock was answered by Margaret and Nelly, both of whom denied that they had seen the old woman, and who made a great show of resenting the very suggestion that they would allow such a person into their house. As the three women argued, Hare appeared from the inner room and called Peggy in. He told the girl that her mother had indeed been there, but had gone off to Mid Calder. Hare was hospitable and, when Burked joined them, the whisky bottle was produced, and within hours Peggy was reunited with her mother—on the anatomists' slab at No 10 Surgeons' Square.

FIVE

Daft Jamie's Last Fight

Fourteen murders in ten months, not a breath of suspicion, and only one alarm when they brought Mary Paterson's body to Surgeons' Square. Burke and Hare must have begun to imagine that they enjoyed a charmed life, or at the very least that they were skilled in murder beyond the powers of detection.

In the streets of the city from the West Port to Canongate with all the closes and wynds that lay between, there were many characters from whom to select victims. Prostitutes had already proved a good source of supply, but there were all the members of that odd and misshapen band who begged or sold cheap goods round the doors. Burke and Hare watched them and marked down those who were suitable, among them 'Daft Jamie' Wilson, a feeble-minded lad of 18 with a slightly deformed foot who found a living in the streets of Edinburgh.

Jamie had no need to sleep in the streets; his mother had a house but he would not live with her because she had beaten him one day. The story of Jamie's leaving home is that once, when he did not return by nightfall, his mother became worried and went out in search of him. Jamie returned in the meantime, and found the door locked so he broke it open. He was hungry and, in his search for something to eat, pulled over a cupboard and smashed his mother's crockery. Mrs Wilson took a leather strap to the boy when she discovered the havoc in her house, and Jamie walked out and would never stay with her again.

From then on he earned a copper wherever he could and slept in whichever part of the city he happened to find himself at night.

It was a hard life, but no worse than it had been when he lived with his widowed mother.

Even in Edinburgh in 1828, a city unacquainted with pity, Jamie evoked sympathy and people gave him food and clothes. Nevertheless, he limped around the city barefoot and in rags because, he explained, if he wore the good clothes which people gave him, they would think he was well enough off and give him nothing more.

Jamie's prized possession was his box of snuff and brass snuff spoon with seven holes which he said represented the days of the week. He named the middle one Sunday.

Jamie was daft, but he was cleaner in his person than most of his companions in the streets; he was amiable and would entertain his friends with a song or a joke. Many of the latter sound to us like forerunners of the music hall humour of the second half of the century and possibly they were not Jamie's jokes at all, but simply stories then current in Edinburgh, which were attributed to him in the many pamphlets and tales of his life which circulated at the time.

"What month do ladies talk least?" is a sample of Jamie's riddles. Answer, "February, because there are fewer days in it."

Jamie's one talent lay in being able to work out the day on which a certain date would fall, but otherwise he was a figure of fun to everyone—especially to the children of the town. Jamie was a tall lad, and strong, but completely without the will to fight. A scrap of a child would square up to him in the street and offer to fight him, but Jamie would simply look down on the boy and say that only bad boys fought. The boy would then hit him, and Jamie would run away shouting, "That wisna' sair, man. Ye canna' catch me!"

A handful of boys would then pursue him screaming, "Ye're daft, Jamie; ye're daft", and Jamie would stop and ask pathetically, "What way dae ye ca' me daft?"

"Because ye are," they would answer.

"I'm no', though: as sure as daith I'm no' daft at a'."

"Ye are, ye are," the discordant chant continued until Jamie took to his heels and ran.

53

Oddly enough the only person with whom Jamie was ever known to fight was his best friend, Robert Kirkwood, who was known in the town as 'Bobby Awl'. Their single quarrel was over a sheep's head which a butcher had given to Jamie and which Bobby fancied. Jamie won the fight, but at the cost of a bloodied nose.

Generally, Jamie accepted Bobby's tricks and cheating without protest—even on the day when Bobby stole his drink. The boys had managed between them to gather together enough money to buy a drink each, and when the whisky was set before them Bobby said to his friend, "Hae ye seen the twa dugs fechting in the street?"

"I saw nae dugs fechting," replied Jamie.

"It's a grand fecht though," Bobby insisted, "and has lasted half an hour. It's weel worth your seeing—ye'd better gang to the door and see it."

Jamie went to the door, but soon returned to say he could see no fight.

"They'll be dune then," his friend explained.

Suddenly Jamie noticed his empty glass.

"But what's come o' the whisky?" he asked.

"Oh, man, ye bade sae lang I couldna' wait," replied Bobby.

When Jamie recounted the story, friends asked what revenge he took on Bobby for this mean trick, Jamie only replied, "What could ye say to puir Bobby? He's daft, ye ken."

The stories of 'Daft Jamie's' life are many: a number of stories are also told of how he met his death.

Burke's own version blames Lucky Hare for enticing Jamie to Tanner's Close one morning early in October 1828, and leaving him there with Hare while she went out in search of Burke. She found her husband's confederate in Rymer's shop and asked him to buy her a drink, during which procedure she stamped on his foot as a signal that there was a subject at Tanner's Close and that he should go there at once.

Burke hurried to the house and found Hare trying to persuade Jamie to accept some whisky, which he was stubbornly refusing, for Jamie had decided not to accept Hare's drink and nothing would make him change his mind. Indeed, Burke says that Jamie drank hardly a glass of whisky that morning. After a while Jamie lay down on the bed in the little back room to have a sleep, and Hare lay down beside him, leaning on one elbow. Burke sat on the edge of the bed while Mrs Hare discreetly went out, locked the door of the house behind her and slipped the key back underneath it. Hare lay until he thought Jamie was asleep, then leapt on top of the boy and covered his nose and mouth. Jamie was strong—unnaturally strong—and he fought back so hard that he and Hare rolled on to the floor. After a long struggle, during which Burke held the lad's hands and feet, Jamie's resistance weakened and he was overwhelmed.

A second version of the murder, supposedly based on Hare's testimony and bearing all the marks of the story Hare would put out, claims that Burke met Jamie searching for his mother in the Grassmarket one morning and took him to Tanner's Close where he plied him with drink until he fell asleep on the floor. Burke was anxious to get on with the murder and ignored Hare's advice to wait because the boy was too strong. Burke leapt on top of the boy, but Jamie shook him off and soon had Burke screaming for help. Hare tripped Jamie up and, as the lad fell, the two leapt on him and fought with him until Jamie had strength to struggle no more.

Burke suffered from a cancerous sore in a testicle, and popular gossip said that this was caused by a bite from Jamie during this struggle. However, like so many of the stories which circulated and were generally believed at the time, that is not true: the sore had given him pain for a long time and would probably have caused his death before long.

They stripped the body of its clothes, which Burke took to Constantine and his children who were running in rags, and a baker later saw Constantine wearing a pair of trousers which he had given to Daft Jamie. Hare took the snuffbox and spoon from Jamie's pocket, and kept the box but gave the spoon to Burke.

Jamie was murdered about noon. Later in the day they took the body to Surgeons' Square and collected £10, since the new season of lectures had just begun and the doctors were paying the winter rate for subjects. Burke refused to pay Lucky a penny, probably because he was tired of doing a half share of the work, yet giving £6 to the Hares for every £4 he kept to himself, and she was so angry that she did not speak to him for three weeks.

The following morning one of the students recognised the body as Daft Jamie, whom he had seen alive and well in the street only two weeks earlier. Burke and Hare had run a terrible risk in choosing a character as well known as Jamie. Their luck held, however, for Paterson, the doorman, claims that Dr Knox denied that this was Jamie, but began the dissection of the body immediately.

SIX

Last Shot for the Doctor

In 1828 Hallowe'en fell on a Friday at the end of an autumn so mild that strawberries were on sale in Edinburgh at two shillings a basket only a week before. The corn and potato harvest had been good, and oysters were in such abundance that prices fell alarmingly and the oyster fishers could scarcely earn a living. During the last week of October, however, the weather changed, and a succession of thick fogs hid the city, so that when one looked south from Princes Street it seemed as if the ancient Scottish capital had been spirited away, castle and all.

In Edinburgh it was 'preaching week', the week of prayer and sermons in preparation for the November communion services of the Presbyterian Church, so everyone had been harangued with threats of hellfire; indeed, some thought it was among them when a beam fractured with a resounding crack during a service in a church in the Potterrow.

On the morning of Hallowe'en the fog cleared, and by nine o'clock everyone was at work as usual. Those like William Burke who had no regular employment were thinking about their first drink of the day—a thirst which took Burke to Rymer's shop in the West Port. He was a regular customer there, and well respected, for he liked his dram and always had money in his pocket to pay for it. It crossed Mr Rymer's mind from time to time that the legacy, which Mr Burke said he had inherited in the spring, had lasted well. However, one did not question where a customer's money came from: one was just thankful in these hard times that he had any money at all.

As Burke talked to Rymer's shop boy, William Noble, the door opened and a woman pushed her way in. She was old but not aged, small but not tiny, and poor but not in rags. She wore a cheap flower-printed dress over a red-striped petticoat, which looked more like a nightgown, and her head was covered with a scarf. She thrust her hand across the counter towards the boy and asked for alms.

The accent was Irish—the rich, clipped brogue of the north-west, and Burke recognised it as that of his home county. He turned and examined the woman carefully from head to foot, then smiled and asked where she was from.

The stranger also recognised Burke's accent as an Ulster one, and it brought a breath of home which was welcome in this cold city of flat vowels and sing-song sentence endings. She replied to his question: from Donegal . . . a place called Innisowen.

Innisowen! Burke knew it well, for it was the very spot to which his mother belonged, although he himself had been born in the neighbouring county of Tyrone. He bought her a dram, and talked enthusiastically about the 'ould' country. The woman told him her name was Mary Docherty.

Docherty, indeed! Sure now, that was his mother's name . . . they must be kinsmen. But what brought her to these inhospitable parts?

Mary, now assured of a sympathetic ear, told her story. She had come from Glasgow in search of her son, found him, but he had disappeared again and now she was renewing the search. She had no money, and had not breakfasted, so she was glad to accept her kinsman's invitation to his home where his wife had a pot of porridge on the hob. Burke dismissed Mary's protests that she had nothing to give in return by telling her that a plate of porridge was little enough to offer a relative in such a time of worry and distress. Sure even if she had money he wouldn't take it, so he would be obliged if she would say no more and accept his meagre hospitality.

Burke's house was only a few yards from Rymer's shop and after more liquor and talk of Ireland, he led the way there. Mrs Docherty (as he continued to call her although her married name was Campbell) took in every detail of his person as he turned to talk to her— neat little man of no more than five feet tall; plumpish, but with a strong neck and wire-thin arms. She noted his tight lips and black eyes which bored into her like a drill as he spoke. He was not a powerful man, to be sure, and seemed much more fitted to be a dancing master than a cobbler, which he had told her was his trade.

Burke turned into a 'land', and beckoned her to follow. He led the way along a passage, down a stair, and turned right into a dank, pitch-black corridor with a door at the end of it. Burke opened the door and called to Mrs Docherty to enter. Mary found herself in a basement flat which consisted of a single room, and not a very large one at that. It was only a little lighter than the passage because its one window looked out on to a wall above which a fragment of sky was visible. The place was clean enough, but it had few furnishings—a chair, a stool or two, a wooden framed bed, and a pile of straw at its foot to provide an additional place to sleep. The floor, which was sanded, was strewn with cobbler's tools, pieces of leather, and piles of boots and shoes. On the hob of the fireplace, which was set into the wall opposite the door, stood the pot of porridge of which William had spoken.

There were several people in the room, and Burke introduced Mary to them. The first he told her was his wife Nelly, who welcomed the newcomer warmly. The others were James Gray and his wife Ann, who was related to Nelly. Burke ordered Mrs Gray to fetch a plate for their guest, and they all ate. During the meal Mrs Docherty told the story of the meeting with Burke in Rymer's shop, and of the chance which had brought two relatives together so far from home. Mary was well aware of her good fortune and was in no hurry to leave. When she did make a move to go she was pressed to stay, so she settled down and drank, talked, and removed her petticoat and washed it. She made herself quite at home.

During the morning Burke went out to buy more drink for the party which would be held that evening to celebrate Hallowe'en— at least that was what he told Mary Docherty. In fact, he had chosen her as his next victim, and was searching for his friend

59

William Hare to lay his devilish plan. He found Hare in Rymer's shop and whispered to him, "I have got a shot for the doctors". Hare needed no more explanation: he knew exactly what Burke meant and was ready to fall in with the scheme.

While Mrs Docherty washed her clothes and Burke laid his plans, life continued normally in the dark basement room. Two neighbours, Mrs Lawrie and Mrs Connoway, who lived in similar flats on the same floor, visited the house, the young relative John Brogan dropped in, and all the time the whisky bottle circulated. With every hour the party became jollier, and Burke pressed Mrs Docherty to stay. To make his plan possible he had to get rid of the Grays, and he did this by accusing them of quarrelling (which no doubt was true), and telling them they would have to leave— but he was not a hard man, so he had arranged for them to go to the house of his friends Mr and Mrs Hare. Towards evening he took them to Hare's house in Tanner's Close, not far away, and he himself prepared a bed for them.

Mrs Docherty was now left alone in the darkening house with Nelly, but she did not mind because the whisky had begun to befuddle her head. In due course Nelly left, too, and the old woman wandered into Mrs Connoway's house which opened off the passage leading to Burke's room. The door was left open, and one by one the conspirators gathered there—first Hare and his wife, then Nelly, who produced a bottle of whisky from under her apron and passed it round. Hare and Nelly led the old lady in a dance until she hurt her feet and had to sit down. Despite her sore feet Mary had not enjoyed herself so much for years. Indeed she had become very affectionate towards William Burke and would not leave until he returned. When she saw him pass along the corridor she followed him into his house.

In Burke's room the party continued with verve: the men drank, their wives danced and the old woman sang. Mrs Lawrie and the Connoways went to bed early because they could not lie late in the morning as members of the Burke household were able to do, but they heard the revels next door as they dropped off to sleep.

Burke now put his scheme into action. He had already called at Rymer's and asked the shop boy to set a tea chest aside for him, and then at ten o'clock he slipped across the street to the house of David Paterson, porter at Dr Robert Knox's anatomy school, but was told he was out. Between eleven o'clock and midnight the sleeping households in the basement heard a disturbance, which did not surprise them, considering the amount of whisky that had been consumed during the day and evening. Hugh Alston, who lived on the first floor of the 'land', also heard it as he and his wife returned home towards midnight. He heard two men fighting, and a woman's voice cry, "Murder", so he bundled his wife upstairs towards their home and went to investigate. At the foot of the basement stairs he stopped and listened. It was all over within a minute or two—the quarrelling; the woman's cry of "For God's sake get the police, there is murder here"; and the noise as if from a person or animal that has been strangled.

Had Alston gone a few yards farther he would have discovered Nelly and Margaret standing in the passage: had he gone into the room he would have found that the fight between Burke and Hare had been contrived to give them an opportunity of seizing Mary Docherty when she intervened, and holding their hands over her nose and mouth to suffocate her. But Alston did not go far enough. He dithered for a moment, then rushed into the street to find a patrolling policeman. Again he hesitated too long and in the end did nothing. In the distance he saw a policeman but could not catch up with him, so he returned to the stairway and listened. All was quiet now, and he assumed that he had overheard nothing more than a drunken family quarrel, which was now over.

As Alston climbed the stairs to his house Burke crept up from the basement and across the road again in search of Paterson. He found Dr Knox's porter just returning home, and brought him back to the room where the murder had taken place less than an hour before. Burke pointed to the pile of straw and whispered:

"There lies a subject for the doctors tomorrow."

Paterson knew quite well that he referred to a body, but he did not want to linger in this house with four drunken people and a corpse. He told Burke to see the doctor in the morning and left hurriedly.

Next morning, Saturday, 1st November, drinking began again

as soon as everyone was awake. By nine o'clock the house was filled with Burke, Nelly, Hares, Grays, Brogan, Mrs Connoway and Mrs Lawrie. Indeed, the presence of all the Hallowe'en revellers served to emphasise the absence of yesterday's newcomer. Mrs Lawrie was the first to ask what had become of Mary Docherty.

Nelly feigned anger: "I kicked the damned bitch's backside out of the door for she was making ower free with my William."

To Brogan she was more forthcoming.

"She was fashous," said Nelly sharply, "a very troublesome woman. First she wanted warm water, then cold, and then she asked for a flannel clout and soap to wash herself with. The two men began fighting and the old woman roared out, 'Murder', so I gave her a kick in the backside and set her to the door—the old Irish limmer."

In spite of the apparent wrath of his wife, Burke was buoyant and quarrelsome. He continued to drink, and waved the whisky bottle around him throwing its contents on to the ceiling, on to himself, and around the bed. The reason, he said, was to empty the bottle so that he could buy some more—which he promptly did—but on the way he again called on Paterson who sent him directly to Dr Knox.

When Mrs Gray approached the straw to search for her child's stockings and later to get potatoes from the store beneath the bed, Burke shouted roughly at her to keep away. When he went out he ordered Brogan to stay guard by the straw and let no one near it. It did not occur to him that this would arouse suspicion and make Ann Gray seize the first chance to look under the straw.

Mrs Gray went about the business of cleaning the house and bided her time until Brogan deserted his post towards nightfall. she hurried to the corner and lifted the straw—first she saw an arm, and then, when she pulled back more straw, the naked body of Mary Docherty. She called her husband and together they lifted the head and looked at the blood-stained face. They were sure that the woman had not died naturally, and decided to flee as fast as they could. The two gathered together their few belongings and hurried out of the house.

On the stair they encountered Nelly who asked where they were going. Gray answered her question with another.

"What's this you've got in the house?" he demanded.

"What do you mean?" asked Nelly.

"I suppose very well that you know what it is," replied Gray, and Mrs Burke realised that the secret of the straw had been discovered. She fell to her knees. "Hold your tongue and I'll give you five or six shillings," she babbled. "Keep quiet about what you have seen and it will be worth £10 a week to you."

"God forbid that I would be worth that," retorted Gray, "for I couldna' keep it on my conscience."

Nelly repeated her offer to Ann Gray, who also refused.

"What do you mean by bringing your family into disgrace in such a way?" demanded Mrs Gray.

"My God," cried Nelly, "I cannot help it."

"You can surely help it or you wouldna' stay in the house."

With that the Grays stormed into the street, pursued by Nelly. The next person they met was Margaret Hare, who persuaded them all to be quiet and go to a public house where they could talk things over, but talk and drinks had no effect—Gray was determined to go to the police.

As the Grays set out to report their discovery to the police, the two women hurried off to warn Burke and Hare. Mrs Hare was sent to collect the tea chest from Rymer's, while Burke hurried to Allison's Close, off the Cowgate, to fetch John McCulloch, a porter. McCulloch saw what was being put into the tea chest, but he knew how to hold his tongue. He roped the chest and carried it, on Burke's instructions, out by the back way, over the waste ground at the back of the 'land', along the Cowgate and up the High School Wynd to No 10 Surgeons' Square. Burke and Hare followed, and Nelly and Mrs Hare lurked in the background. At Surgeons' Square the chest was handed over to Paterson and a little procession of Burke and Hare, Nelly and Margaret, McCulloch and Paterson, made its way to the doctor's house at Newington Place. There Paterson collected £5 *on account* and divided it equally between Burke and Hare. McCulloch was paid five shillings, and sent home.

While this little caravan was heading home from Newington another was making its way from the police station beside St Giles Cathedral to the West Port. James Gray had arrived at the police office about seven o'clock and told his tale to Sergeant-Major John Fisher, one of the detectives there. Together with a police patrolman, John Findlay, they set out for Burke's house but found it empty. A servant girl told of the chest being carried out the back door and the police were contemplating their next move when Burke and Nelly returned. Fisher asked Burke what had become of his lodgers.

"This is one of them, but I had to put him out because of his bad conduct," said William, pointing to Gray.

"And what about the little woman who was here yesterday?" asked Fisher.

"She's away . . . she left the house about seven o'clock this morning."

"Did anybody see her go?"

"Surely officer; William Hare was here when she left."

"Anybody else, Mr Burke?"

Burke's tone grew insolent. "A number of others will swear they saw her leave, officer. Quite a few, you may be sure."

"Then I'll just take a look around if you don't mind."

Burke merely gestured, and looked sullenly on as the police officers examined the straw and the bed. Fisher held up some blood-stained bedclothes, and asked Nelly how the blood came to be there. Nelly had a ready answer. "A woman lay there in childbirth not a fortnight since," she said, "and the bed has not been washed since."

"And what about the old woman who was here yesterday, Mrs Burke?"

"Oh, I could find her for you rightly, officer. She lives in the Pleasance: I ken her weel. Indeed, I saw her in the vennel near the West Port only this night. She apologised for her conduct on Hallowe'en."

"At what time did she leave your house?" the officer asked.

"Seven o'clock at night, it was."

The police officer spotted the fateful error—Burke had said

seven *in the morning*, but Nelly said seven *in the evening*. However, he gave no indication that he suspected them of lying.

"I'm sure it is all personal spite that has stirred this up," he said, "but maybe you'd better come up to the police office with me and get it all cleared up."

The two agreed—they could hardly do otherwise, and after all the body had been well and truly disposed of in Dr Knox's cellar, and without a body there could be no case against them.

But there was a body, and on Sunday morning the police found it at No 10 Surgeons' Square. Fisher unroped the chest, and there crammed mercilessly into the tiny space, lay the remains of a woman—an old woman just as Gray had described.

Gray was sent for and confirmed that the body was Mrs Docherty. His identification was corroborated in due course by Mrs Lawrie, Mrs Connoway, and a number of others who had been at Burke's house on Hallowe'en. As clothing belonging to the old woman was found and the evidence against them became firmer the Burkes blustered and denied all knowledge of the woman. When the Hares were brought to the police office and put in separate cells, they too claimed that they had never seen the woman.

But all Edinburgh knew by this time that a terrible murder had been committed, and that the Burkes and Hares were deeply implicated. The wild rumours which began to run through the narrow streets of the old town and down the Mound to the new one were in marked contrast to the restraint of Monday's *Evening Courant* which reported the "Extraordinary Occurrence" of the discovery of Mary Docherty's body. The newspaper hinted at "singular circumstances" and suspicions that the body had been sold to the anatomists. Men and women in the street were more open: they whispered "Mass murder". How many others had been done away with to satisfy the doctors in Surgeons' Square, they asked, and that night all Edinburgh began to look twice at a stranger. People racked their brains to remember who had vanished without explanation or farewell during recent months—and there were many.

65

SEVEN

The Strongest Suspicion

On Monday, 3rd November the police were very satisfied: they had a body, they had witnesses, and they had four suspects in custody. It seemed an excellent case—at first. Unfortunately the method stumbled on by the murderers quite by accident was so cunning that it was difficult to say whether Mary Docherty had died by violence or not.

The first person to examine the body was Alexander Black, an old-fashioned medical man, who had been surgeon to the police for nearly twenty years. During that time he had seen the bodies of many victims of murder by strangulation and many others who had been suffocated accidentally through vomiting after drinking. Black had known as many as half a dozen such accidental cases to be brought in during a single night—so many, indeed, that he did not know which to attend to first.

Black gave it as his private opinion that Mary had died from violence, but medically he could not be sure of the cause. His opinion was confirmed by Robert Christison, Professor of Medical Jurisprudence at Edinburgh University, and another Edinburgh doctor, William Newbigging, who carried out a post mortem examination on the Sunday and Monday. There were a few bruises on Mrs Docherty's limbs, but no external marks on the neck or face to indicate how breathing had been obstructed. The neck was loose and the ligaments between two of the vertebrae of the neck were torn and a little fluid blood was effused beneath the spinal investing sheath and among the muscles of the neck and back. Christison and Newbigging had not been told the story of the disturbance, or of the cries of 'Murder', so they wondered whether death had been due to the head being forcibly bent over the breast. After experimenting they decided that the cervical spinal injury had been caused soon after death, most likely when the body was put into the tea chest. The bruises, they believed, were inflicted not long before death, by blows or kicks, or just as probably by falls or by tumbling against hard objects.

Every appearance pointed to accidental suffocation: if Mary Docherty died by violence, then she had been smothered and not strangled. Christison admitted later: "This evidence was, of course, insufficient to bear out a charge of murder, though such as to raise the strongest suspicion." The strongest suspicion, however, was not sufficient to convince a jury.

While the surgeons were carrying out their autopsy the police were taking statements from the four prisoners, from neighbours, and from all others who had been involved. Unfortunately, the process of the law succeeded in suppressing the statements of the Hares, but the declarations of Burke and Nelly McDougal were read at the trial.

On Monday, 3rd November, the Sheriff Substitute of Midlothian, George Tait, heard William Burke's statement—and a highly improbable tale it proved to be! On Hallowe'en he, Nelly and the Grays were in the house at the West Port, said Burke in his most plausible manner. It was a perfectly normal day during which he busied himself mending shoes. At about six o'clock he was standing at the entry to the 'land' when a man muffled in a greatcoat came up to him and asked where he could have a pair of shoes mended. Burke took him into his house and gave him an old pair to wear while he repaired those which the man had just taken off. While Burke worked the stranger paced about the room, and remarked that it was a quiet place. Then he said he had a box which he would like to leave in Burke's care for a short time. Burke agreed, and the man went out and returned a few minutes later with a box tied with a rope. Burke sat looking out the window as the man put the box down. Then he heard sounds of the box being unroped and the straw being rustled. The stranger changed into his own shoes, paid sixpence for the repair, and left.

William was curious and, when he found the box to be empty, he lifted the straw and saw a body lying underneath it. When the stranger returned Burke told him it was wrong of him to have brought a body to his house, and ordered him to pack it in the box again and take it away. The man promised to do so shortly, and disappeared again. But the stranger did not return that night, and the body continued to lie underneath the straw.

On the Saturday morning, continued Burke, he went to Rymer's shop and there met an old Irishwoman who was probably a distant relation. He took her home, gave her breakfast, and allowed her to sit at the fire, smoking her pipe until mid-afternoon when she said she was going to the New Town to beg food. He did not see her again.

At six o'clock the stranger returned with a porter whom Burke knew by sight because he had a stance at the head of the Cowgate or the foot of Candlemaker Row. The two men repacked the body in the box, and the stranger said they were taking it to Surgeons' Square, but Burke took him to see David Paterson who had some connection with the doctors there. Burke accompanied the stranger to Surgeons' Square and, when they had delivered the body, Paterson paid some money to the man, and £2 10s to Burke.

On returning home he found the neighbours had raised a hue and cry over a body which had been found in the house, and as he went out in search of a policeman he met Findlay and the other police officer on their way in.

He had been shown a body at the police office, which he thought was the one which the stranger had hidden in the straw, but it bore no likeness to Mary Docherty. Burke was prepared to agree to anything that would help his case: he named the stranger as William Hare and the porter as John McCulloch.

The Sheriff-Substitute then interrogated Nelly McDougal, and clearly no story had been agreed between the two. Nelly said that on the morning of Hallowe'en a woman had wandered into the house, the worse of drink, and asked to light her pipe at the fire. She then asked for soap to wash her cap and nightgown. The woman did her washing in their house, and when the clothes were dry Mrs Gray ironed them for her. The woman, who said her name was Mary, told them she was searching for her son, but she was hungry and glad to accept breakfast and a dram from them. At two o'clock Mary went away to Saint Mary's Wynd in search of her son again.

Nelly then told the story of sending the Grays away, of the drinking, and how Burke and Hare fell asleep on the bed while she and Margaret Hare slept on the floor. On the Saturday they all went about their tasks until evening when Mrs Gray raised a noise about a body in the straw.

Nelly was shown the body but refused to identify it as Mary— the woman who had visited them had dark hair, she said, while that of the dead woman at the police office was grey.

She explained that the blood on the pillowslip was her own— Burke had struck her and made her nose bleed. The blood on the sheet was also hers, because this was the time of her menstruation.

Nelly was unable to sign the statement since the last thing she declared was that she was illiterate.

A week later Burke made a second statement, correcting certain facts in his first one. Now he admitted that Mary Docherty came to the house on Friday and not Saturday, and that after she left at three, the others celebrated Hallowe'en until they were "pretty hearty". That night Mary returned and drank with them until late. He and Hare fell out and began to fight, and by the time the womenfolk had separated them the old woman had disappeared. They searched for her and found her lying among the straw apparently dead. On Hare's suggestion they stripped the clothes from the body and agreed to sell it to the surgeons.

The following evening he tried to find Paterson but Knox's doorkeeper was out, so instead he fetched McCulloch and took the body to No 10 Surgeons' Square.

By this time Burke had been told something of the doctor's findings, for he added that force was necessary to get the body into the chest so that they may have hurt the neck a little.

Nelly had little to add to her statement. On the same day she said that between three and four o'clock on the Friday afternoon Mary insisted on having soap to wash herself with and asked for tea several times. Nelly told the woman that she could not be bothered with her any more and pushed her out of the door. She never saw her again.

The medical evidence and the statements of the prisoners did not take the lawyers very far forward. They certainly did not add up to a case which would convince a jury.

Edinburgh took the news of the arrests quietly, if not calmly. The newspapers said singularly little. The *Evening Courant* had carried the bare story of Mary Docherty's death on Monday, 3rd November, but very soon rumours began to sweep the town—rumours of wholesale murder and sale of bodies to the doctors for dissection. Names of possible victims were whispered, and friends and relatives of any person who had disappeared in the past twelve months began to make enquiries around the town.

On the following Thursday, 6th November, the *Courant* reported: "A great number of rumours have gone abroad of individuals having of late disappeared in an unaccountable manner; one of them, however, a sort of half-witted lad called Daft Jamie was seen on Monday, not far from Lasswade with a basket selling small ware . . ."

The same issue of the *Courant* reported that the four suspects had given very contradictory accounts of the manner of Docherty's death. Hare said that Brogan struck her and killed her, and Burke was alleged to have admitted to helping to dispose of the body.

One of those who listened to the rumours with horror was Janet Brown who had never given up the search for her friend Mary Paterson. She stopped Constantine Burke in the street several times during the summer and asked what had become of Mary. At first he said she had gone to Glasgow with a packman, but when she persisted with her questioning he became angry and stormed, "How the hell can I tell about you sort of folk? You are here today and away tomorrow."

Once he gave a more disturbing answer: "I am often out upon my lawful business, and how can I answer for all that takes place in my house in my absence?"

Janet was far from satisfied, and she went to the police when she learned of the arrest of Burke and Hare. She identified the four prisoners as the last people with whom she had seen her friend alive, and she identified Mary's clothes among those found in Burke's house. Janet was now sure she knew the fate of her friend.

Mary Paterson's clothes were not the only pieces of evidence which the police found in Burke's house. They were able to identify clothes belonging to Mary Docherty, and Daft Jamie's snuff spoon and clothes as well.

Walter Abernethy, a young sailor from Scalloway in Shetland, had a tale to hand down to his children and his children's children when he heard of the murders. Earlier in the year he had come ashore from his ship at Leith and there he met a stranger who invited him to visit a lodging house in Tanner's Close, where a lot of Shetland people congregated. "In fact, in our lodging house hardly an evening passes without someone from Shetland calling," the stranger told him. A few nights later Walter went to Tanner's Close, and there he was shown into a room by himself. A woman came in carrying a bottle and a glass. She poured a drink which she handed to him. "Drink up," she said, and added in a whisper, "and run for your life." Walter did not hesitate: he took to his heels and ran from the close with the noise of pursuing feet behind him. He thought at the time that he had narrowly escaped being beaten and robbed, but when he heard about the West Port murders, he realised that his escape had been from something much more sinister.

A woman recalled how she had arrived in Edinburgh in July, accompanied by her two children, to search for her husband. In the West Port she met a man wearing a cobbler's leather apron, and he invited her to his house, where his wife made tea while he went in search of the husband. When the woman became uneasy and wanted to leave, the cobbler's wife invited her to rest on the bed and fussed over the children. The woman would not stay, but she remembered the incident three months later, and felt she had had a narrow escape.

There was no doubt in the minds of the mob about the guilt of the four prisoners. Indeed, there was no doubt either in the mind of the Lord Advocate, Sir William Rae, the man with whom lay the final decision of whether to prosecute or not. Sir William realised, however, that the medical evidence was woefully thin, and, apart from a reasonable amount of circumstantial evidence, he had little else on which to base a prosecution. He could not be sure of obtaining a conviction on this evidence, and yet he felt that he must break up the ghoulish conspiracy. In the end he decided that the only course open to him was to persuade one of the gang to turn king's evidence on his friends. But which? Rae thought the matter out carefully and decided that Burke was the ring-leader, so must be convicted at all costs. Technically, Nelly could give evidence against him since she was not legally married to him, but it was obvious in any case that she would not. It was no good choosing Margaret Hare because, while she could give evidence against both Burke and Nelly, she could not testify against her husband. That left Hare, the more stupid of the two men, and the more likely to strike a bargain with the authorities. Rae made the right choice.

On 1st December Hare was interviewed and given an assurance that "if he would disclose the facts relative to the case of Docherty, and to such other crimes of a similar nature, committed by Burke, of which he was cognisant, he should not be brought to trial on account of his accession to any of these crimes".

Hare at once 'sang' loud and long: his confession provided a rich harvest of witnesses as information tumbled from his lips about murder after murder. And all the time he made Burke out to be the chief participant.

At last the Lord Advocate was reasonably sure that he had evidence on which no jury could fail to convict in three cases—the murders of Mary Paterson, Daft Jamie Wilson and Mary Docherty. In all three cases clothes belonging to the victims had been found in Burke's possession, and in that of Mary Paterson, Janet Brown could identify Burke.

A week later William Burke was served with an indictment for the murders of the two women and Daft Jamie, and Helen McDougal was charged on the same indictment with one of the murders—that of Mary Docherty. In making sure of his case the Lord Advocate had paid a high price—he had given guarantees of immunity to William Hare and he had virtually abandoned all hope of prosecuting Margaret Hare.

72

Imagine Burke's feelings when he heard this! Imagine the feelings of the Edinburgh mob! The trial was set for Christmas Eve—an incredible choice of date to us in Scotland today, but not unusual in the Scotland of 1828. It was less than three weeks away, and the populace sat back to see justice catch up with the West Port murderers.

EIGHT

The Price of Justice

During the days leading up to Wednesday, 24th December, the people of Edinburgh talked of nothing but the impending trial. The first of a large flood of broadsheets and verses began to appear, prejudging the case and even bringing accusations of guilt against people who were not under arrest. The case was tried a thousand times in the streets, and excitement became so intense as Christmas week opened that the authorities were terrified lest the mob might hang Burke from a lamp-post. They had good reason to be afraid, for it had happened before, and there were many in Edinburgh at that moment who vowed that it would happen again.

At six o'clock on the evening of 23rd December the police were reinforced with an additional three hundred men, and infantry at the Castle and cavalry at Piershill were put on the alert to march into the city at a moment's notice. At dead of night the prisoners were brought secretly from the Calton Jail to Parliament House, where the trial was to be held, and lodged in the cells until morning.

The streets around were bursting with people long before daybreak as thousands struggled to get into the building which was far too small to hold more than fraction of the number who sought admittance.

The High Court of Justiciary in those days met in the great Parliament Hall, which had once been the meeting place of the Scottish Parliament. This hall, which had witnessed the passing of the treaty uniting Scotland and England in 1707, was divided

into two parts by a screen. The High Court sat in the southern
end, while the northern one was used as the Sheriff Court and
as a kind of lobby filled with taverns and shops. It was a long
narrow building, stone-walled, and with a black oak roof glowering
down on the scene. As a courtroom it was dark, cold, and dam-
nably uncomfortable! On Christmas Eve, 1828, it was far too small
as well.

Members of the press were led to their seats a little before eight,
to sit alone and cold until nine o'clock when members of the
Faculty of Advocates and Writers to the Signet were admitted. It
was customary on all great judicial occasions at that time for half
of the space in the court to be reserved for these legal luminaries,
and on this occasion every member who could availed himself of
the privilege. As a result there was precious little room for the
public.

William Burke and Helen McDougal were brought into the
court at nine-forty, and there they sat while officials bustled about
and took their places. Burke looked small, with a waif-like appearance rather than that of a monster, and Nelly was generally
regarded as less attractive than ever, a small grey velvet bonnet
framing the large bones of her face. Her bonnet looked as sad as
her countenance, and as worn as her printed cotton shawl and
dress. She stooped as she walked into the court, and as one commentator noted, had "nothing peculiar in her appearance, except
the ordinary look of extreme poverty and misery common to
unfortunate females of the same degraded class". Only one reporter
had a good word to say about her appearance. "Although the
expression of her features was not upon the whole disagreeable,"
he said, "it frequently assumed a haggard and ghastly appearance
like a person in the jaws of death."

The court met at ten-fifteen, but even before the trial got under
way the atmosphere in the crowded hall was so foul that the
presiding judge, the Lord Justice Clerk, Lord Boyle, ordered a
large window to be opened wide and from then on a current of
cold damp air beat upon the heads of everyone. "The greater part
of the audience being Advocates and Writers to the Signet in
their gowns," wrote one reporter, "these were wrapped round

their heads and, intermingled with various coloured handkerchiefs in every shade and form of drapery, they gave to the visages that were enshrouded under them such a grim and grisly aspect as assimilated them to a college of Monks or Inquisitors, or characters imagined in tales of romance—grouped and contrasted with the costume of the bench and the crowded bar engaged in the trial."

The "crowded bar" comprised the most eminent men of the legal profession in Scotland. Sitting with Lord Boyle were Lords Pitmilly, Meadowbank and Mackenzie, and the prosecution case was to be put by the Lord Advocate, Sir William Rae, and three Advocates-Depute, Archibald Alison, Robert Dundas and Alexander Wood.

The defence fielded a fine team too: the junior counsel had persuaded the greatest advocates to plead the cause of Burke and McDougal. The Dean of the Faculty, Sir James Moncrieff, led for Burke, with the support of Patrick Robertson, Duncan McNeill and David Milne, while Nelly was represented by the great Henry Cockburn, with Mark Napier, Hugh Bruce and George Patton. With such opposing forces, the trial promised the lucky few who had gained admittance, a display of legal fireworks such as is seen only once in a generation.

No sooner had the charges been read out than Moncrieff and Cockburn were on their feet. For Burke it was objected that he was being charged with three murders unrelated and committed at different times and places, and further that his trial was being combined with that of another person who was not even charged with two of the offences. Cockburn protested on this latter point only.

First Patrick Robertson, representing Burke, spoke with what the Lord Advocate described as "talent and zeal"—and what those in the body of the hall must have considered great wordiness. He quoted Sir George Mackenzie and Baron Hume, and turned to cases as far back as 1696. He even cited the practice in English courts, where it was not customary to combine several charges in one indictment. The Lord Advocate responded at equal length, contending that his object in charging McDougal on the same

76

indictment was that if he had tried Burke on his own first, Nelly would have come to the bar faced with substantially the same evidence and her case would certainly have been prejudiced.

The Dean of the Faculty backed Robertson's arguments, and then the Lord Justice Clerk called on the three judges who sat with him to give their opinions. Lord Pitmilly agreed that it was wrong that McDougal should be tried on an indictment which charged three different murders, only one of which she was accused of being concerned in. On the matter of several charges on a single indictment he had more to say. His Lordship had anticipated just such an objection when he first read the charges, and he too had studied past precedents.

> It may not be recollected by counsel, [he began] but there is a case which has not escaped my recollection, where two murders (not indeed unconnected) were charged in one indictment. There were two men killed in the same evening, and the murderer went on trial on that indictment, before me, at Jedburgh. The unhappy man was convicted, and he was executed. I have not the smallest doubt, and I think it would be dangerous if there was a doubt in any quarter whatever on this subject.

His Lordship warmed to his task, and his strong Scottish voice took on a keen cutting edge as he referred to English procedure.

> There may be rules adverse to ours in England on this subject; but our practice has been too well fixed to doubt for a moment, that one individual may be charged with separate acts of the same sort of crime, committed at different times, and in different place, and may go to trial upon such an indictment.

Having established the correctness of the Lord Advocate's case Lord Pitmilly turned to the question of whether it was wise to proceed with all three cases together. He could see the terrible ordeal of three trials in succession, but that was the choice of Burke and, as he had opted for such a course, then the trial should be conducted in that way. Lords Meadowbank and Mackenzie concurred, and the Lord Justice Clerk agreed that the indictments be separated and the public prosecutor be given the choice of which charge to proceed with first.

Rae chose "the third case libelled"—the murder of Mary Docherty, with which both were charged.

The Lord Justice Clerk now turned to the prisoners: "William Burke and Helen McDougal, the indictment having been read in the presence of you both, I ask you, William Burke, are you guilty or not guilty of the third charge contained in this indictment?"

"Not guilty," replied William.

He repeated the question to Nelly.

"Not guilty."

Now the names of the jurors were drawn by ballot.

Nicol Allan, Manager of the Hercules Insurance Company, Edinburgh
John Paton, Builder, Edinburgh
James Trench, Builder, Edinburgh
Peter McGregor, Merchant, Edinburgh
William Bonar, Banker, Edinburgh
James Banks, Agent, Edinburgh
James Melliss, Merchant, Edinburgh
John McFie, Merchant, Leith
Thomas Barker, Brewer, Leith
Henry Fenwick, Grocer, Dunbar
David Brash, Grocer, Leith
David Hunter, Ironmonger, Edinburgh
Robert Jeffrey, Engraver, Edinburgh
William Bell, Grocer, Dunbar
William Robertson, Cooper, Edinburgh

All this had taken a great deal of time; it was midday, but the trial was only just beginning.

The first witness called was James Braidwood, a builder who acted as master of the fire engines of Edinburgh Police. His testimony was brief, as he merely had to confirm that the plan before the court was one which he had made of Burke's house especially for the trial. Mary Stewart, with whom Mrs Docherty had lodged until the morning of Hallowe'en, then told of the old

Irishwoman's departure to search for her son. Mrs Stewart was followed by a succession of other players in the terrible drama of that Hallowe'en night. One by one they filled in the details of the day. Charles McLauchlan, a shoemaker who also lodged with Mrs Stewart, left Mary at the door of his shop at the foot of St Mary's Wynd; William Noble, Rymer's shop boy, saw her leave with Burke; the neighbours in the 'land' where Burke lived, Mrs Ann Connoway and Mrs Janet Lawrie told of the comings and goings all that day and the following morning; Hugh Alston related how he overheard the fight and cries of murder; then the two Patersons, David and his 16-year-old sister, Elizabeth, recounted how Burke had called at their house and how David had visited Burke soon after midnight and—as he now realised— soon after the murder.

John Brogan made a brief appearance, but added little to the prosecution case, and Ann and James Gray followed with their damning testimony about the plan to get them out of the house, and of Burke's curious behaviour which had led them to look under the straw and discover the body. Finally they told how Nelly had tried to silence them with bribes and how they had refused, but had gone to the police instead.

The porter, John McCulloch was called to explain how Burke had approached him on the evening of Saturday, 1st November, and asked him to take a box to Surgeons' Square. Poor McCulloch! He knew what was in the box, but he was reluctant to implicate himself. The questioner came at him ruthlessly.

"Tell us what happened before you carried the box away," the Lord Advocate asked.

"When coming to the end of the bed he (Burke) took some straw off it; he took the sheet and he put it into the box," replied McCulloch.

"And what did he take off next? What did he take out of the straw?"

"I cannot say."

"Did you see him put nothing in the box?"

"The sheet."

79

"Did he take anything like the person of a human body?"

"Yes, I think it was something like the person of a body."

Lord Meadowbank pursued the point. "You have no doubt that it was a body, in short?"

"No, my Lord."

"Did you see anything of it at all?"

"No, my Lord: but when I was going to lift the box, there was something like hair that I felt."

"And did you put that into the box?"

"Yes, and there was a little straw put over it, and he ordered me to take it away."

"Did you put the hair in the box?"

"Yes."

The cross-examination then turned to the police. John Fisher described how Gray had come to him with his tale, how he had been led to find the body at No 10 Surgeons' Square, and how the four—Hares, Burke and McDougal—had reacted when confronted with it.

So the trial ground on. Burke maintained the most perfect self-possession and tranquillity all day, even when the rest of the assembly shuddered at some gruesome detail of evidence. From time to time he talked to Nelly, and occasionally he smiled to himself when he thought some piece of testimony was untrue. He and Nelly took a sip of water from time to time, but by four o'clock in the afternoon they were hungry. Burke asked when they would be given dinner and, when told he would have to wait until six o'clock, he asked if they might have a biscuit or two. At six bread and soup was put before them, and they ate heartily while the trial continued around them.

After darkness fell the streets outside the court remained crowded with anxious groups waiting to question every person who left the building. All day they had hung around, and towards evening the numbers increased until nine o'clock when a gang of men and boys cried that they were going to march on Dr Knox's house. At Surgeons' Square a phalanx of policemen prevented them from doing any damage, so they turned towards the University and broke some windows of Professor Monro's classroom

Surgeons' Square, Edinburgh, in 1829. Dr Knox's rooms are in the centre

The entrance to Hare's house in Tanner's Close, an undated photograph. The house was demolished in 1902

before anyone could stop them. In Parliament Square the crowd lingered until the bitter cold of the December night drove most of them home.

At last word reached the few who refused to leave: they have called William Hare to testify. Inside the court the atmosphere was tense as ears and eyes strained to catch every detail of his evidence and every detail of his face. The soft yellow light cast sinister shadows round the great sombre hall, and Hare's dull eyes appeared dead, and his cheeks sank into great black craters as he talked. As he took the oath he looked utterly loathsome—a reptile rather than a man.

Lord Meadowbank was the first to address him. "Now, we observe that you are at present a prisoner in the Tolbooth of Edinburgh, and from what we know the court understands that you must have had some concern in the transaction now under investigation. It is, therefore, my duty to inform you that whatever share you might have had in that transaction, if you now speak the truth you can never afterwards be questioned in a court of justice, but you are required by the solemn oath you have now taken, to speak the truth, the whole truth, and nothing but the truth; and if you deviate from the truth, or prevaricate in the slightest degree, you may be quite assured that it will not pass without detection; and that the inevitable result will be, the most condign punishment that can be inflicted. You will now answer the questions that are put to you."

Lord Boyle, who presided, told Hare that he was to be questioned about the death of Mary Docherty.

"'T'ould woman, Sir?" Hare enquired brightly. He had been well briefed and knew he had nothing to fear, so he answered readily at first as Lord Meadowbank questioned him about his acquaintance with Burke. When the interrogation turned towards the day of the murder his answers became careful and monosyllabic, but his smile persisted. At times his replies were no more than a series of fragments of sentences unwillingly given, and at other times they were "a silent diabolical nod".

"Were you and Burke drinking together on that day?"

"Yes."

"How much did you drink?"

"A gill."

"Was anybody with you?"

"No."

"Did he tell you about any person being in the house?"

"Yes."

"About what o'clock was it?"

"I could not say; it was the fore part of the day. He took me to his house, and he told me to go down to the house and said that there was an old woman in the house that he was going to murder, and for me to see what they were doing; that he had left some whisky in the house; that he got the woman off the street; and that he thought she would be a good shot to take to the doctors."

The word murder struck the court like forked lightning. At once the Lord Justice Clerk took it up. "Did you not say, sir, in the early part of this statement that he had got a *shot*, and that he was going to *murder* her for the doctor."

Hare continued as if the interruption had never been made, but the Lord Justice Clerk stopped him.

"Did he use the word murder; or did you understand it from the *shot* for the doctors?"

Hare still ignored the question.

"Did he use the word murder?" The question was uttered with force that demanded an answer, and it drove Hare back into that cage of monosyllables from which he must have regretted having emerged.

"Did he use the word murder?"

"No."

"What did you understand by the word shot for the doctors? Did you understand the meaning of it?"

"Yes."

"What was it?"

"That he was going to murder her."

The examinaton then continued, and Hare was allowed to describe his visit to Burke's house where Mary Docherty was busy washing.

82

"She was washing her short gown," explained Hare.

"What colour was it?"

"White and reddish colour—striped."

"Was it like that there?"

A red and white striped garment was handed to the witness who took it and replied quite without feeling as he held it in his hand, "Yes, that is it."

Hare was now led through the evening's proceedings during which, in Hare's words, they became "pretty hearty", and which he claimed culminated in a quarrel between himself and Burke.

"Had you any quarrelling or fighting with Burke?" the Lord Advocate asked.

"He asked what I was doing there in his house," replied Hare. "I told him that Nelly McDougal asked me in to get a dram, and he struck me then."

"Did you strike again?"

"Yes, I did."

"Had you a fight?"

"Yes."

"Now, where were the women during this?"

"They were redding us."

"They came in betwixt you to separate you?"

"Yes. He pushed me down twice on the bed, and the last time I lay on the bed."

"Now when you were fighting, where was the old person?"

"She was sitting by the fire, and she got up and desired Burke to sit down, and she said that she did not want to see Burke abused."

"Did she run out?"

"Yes, she ran out twice to the entry, and cried out for the police."

"What did she call out?"

"It was either murder or police, I could not say which, but it was some of them."

"Well, how was she brought back again?"

"It was Nelly McDougal that fetched her back."

"Both times?"

"Yes."

"Did she then get any push, or fall over on the ground?"

"Yes she did; when we were struggling I pushed her over a little stool."

There Mary lay, unable to rise, and yelled at Burke to stop fighting. At length Hare was thrown on to the bed and he lay still there.

"What did he [Burke] do?" the Lord Advocate asked in a clear, steady voice.

"He stood on the floor; he then got stride-legs on the top of the woman on the floor, and she cried out a little, and he kept in her breath."

"Did he lay himself down upon her?"

"Yes, he pressed down her head with his breast."

Every ear strained to hear the answers.

"She gave a kind of cry, did she?"

"Yes."

"Did she give that more than once?"

"She moaned a little after the first cry."

"How did he apply his hand towards her?"

"He put one hand under the nose, and the other under her chin, under her mouth."

"He stopped her breath, do you mean?"

"Yes."

"Did he continue this for any length of time?"

"I could not exactly say the time; ten or fifteen minutes."

Hare maintained that while this was going on he just sat on a chair and watched. At the first screech when Burke attacked the two women fled from the house and did not return until the murder had been committed. Naturally Hare passed all the blame on to Burke: he claimed that Burke alone stripped the clothes from the body and put it among the straw at the foot of the bed, tying her head and feet together and covering her with a sheet and straw. Burke then went out and returned with Paterson, and after Paterson left they all settled down and slept soundly until morning.

He described the disposal of the body, and the journey to Newington to collect part of the money for it.

As the Lord Advocate completed his examination there was a sudden release of the tension which had built up steadily until the whole courtroom was keyed to an exhausting pitch. As Henry Cockburn rose to take up the questioning everyone relaxed, but within moments they were on the edges of their seats again. Cockburn was then in his fiftieth year and that night he was at the peak of his powers. He began quietly enough with a few innocuous questions about Hare's occupation, but in the midst of this he suddenly flashed at the grinning Hare: "Have you been engaged in supplying bodies to the doctors?"

"Yes."

"Have you been concerned in supplying the doctors with subjects upon other occasions than that you have mentioned?"

The Lord Advocate was on his feet at once. "I object to this course of examination."

Rae realised that Cockburn was well on the way to discrediting Hare's testimony, and thus destroying the prosecutor's case. Cockburn refused to yield. "I request the witness to be withdrawn," he said, and Hare was led from the court. Cockburn now turned to the presiding judge. " I mean to ask him this specific question—'Have you ever been concerned in murders before this one?' I am ready to admit that he is not bound to answer; but I am entitled to put that question. Let him answer it or not as he pleases. It will be for the jury to judge the credit due to him, after seeing how he treats it."

The Lord Advocate retorted that Hare had been warned not to speak of cases other than that involving Mary Docherty, so it was inconceivable how he could be asked about them now. The Lord Justice Clerk agreed, and Lord Meadowbank spoke at some length as to why the question should not be put.

Cockburn was in his element, and sensed Meadowbank's indiscretion in taking sides at this stage.

"Your Lordship will observe," he interposed quietly, "that I have only stated what the proposed question is, but that I have not been heard in support of it. Indeed, I could not have been heard upon it, because it has not yet been objected to by the prosecutor. Nevertheless, one of your Lordships had not only formed, but has expressed an opinion, and a very clear opinion, against it."

He explained carefully his purpose in discrediting Hare's testimony and quoted a recent case where a witness had been asked, "Are you a common prizefighter? Are you the keeper of a gambling table? Did you ever kill a man? And so they go on making him confess or deny or evade the commission of all sorts of iniquities," explained Cockburn, "As a result the judge directed the jury to acquit the accused man."

Counsel and judge argued the competence of questions whose purpose was to discredit a witness, quoting the practice in England and comparing it with the law of Scotland.

Cockburn would not budge an inch; in the end he won permission to put his question. He readily agreed to preface it with a warning that Hare was under the court's protection only in respect of this case, and need not answer. Cockburn did not care, for Hare's silence would be more eloquent than any words he might speak.

Hare chose silence, and other questions which followed were an anti-climax. Undoubtedly Cockburn had stolen the show, and his examination of Hare had brought the trial to life.

Margaret Hare followed, carrying a baby in her arms, but even motherhood did not soften her hard features. The child was suffering from whooping cough and every spasm made it more difficult for her to be heard. It was remarkable how the child managed to cough or cry every time an awkward question was put to its mother, and in the end there were many who thought that the child was being used to cover up those answers which Lucky Hare did not want heard.

Lucky told much the same tale as her husband—the day's events, the fight, and her flight when Burke attacked the old woman. When she and Nelly returned a quarter of an hour later the old woman had vanished.

"Seeing nothing of her what did you suppose?" the Lord Advocate asked.

"I had a supposition that she had been murdered," replied Margaret. "I have seen such tricks before."

Mrs Hare was quite ready to tie the noose round her friend Nelly's neck. She claimed that Nelly told her there was a shot in the house. "That was the very word she used," added Lucky to emphasise the point.

She admitted that she went to Rymer's to get a box for Burke, explaining that he had said he wanted it to hold old shoes. She was even prepared to put her husband in jeopardy. She told the court she had already left him three times, and when Lord Meadowbank questioned her as to why she did not go to the Connoways or to Mrs Lawrie for help she replied that she feared she herself might be murdered; "The thing had happened two or three times before," she said, adding only as an afterthought, "and it was not likely that I should tell a thing to affect my husband."

The prosecutor's case ended with the medical evidence, and if the testimony of the Hares had done little for justice, the doctors' testimony was equally unhelpful. Alexander Black, the police surgeon, was questioned first by Alexander Wood, and repeated his opinion that Mary Docherty died a violent death from suffocation, but that he could not be certain of this in medical terms.

Professor Robert Christison could be no more certain, although he had carried out a much more detailed examination.

"There are certain experiences I have described that would justify a suspicion of death by suffocation, such as a strangulation, smothering, or throttling," he said. "The form I suspected most was throttling, in consequence of the appearance of the cuticle under the chin." But like Black he could not be certain of death by violence.

The case for the prosecution ended with the reading of the various confessions of Burke and Nelly. These were contradictory and obvious prefabrications. They included the highly colourful tale of the man in the greatcoat who left the tea-chest while Burke mended his shoes, and Nelly's pack of lies about the events of the day of the murder and the following day.

No witnesses were called for the defence, so the Lord Advocate began his summing up of the crown case. He went through the evidence, witness by witness, reconstructing the events of the two days of 31st October and 1st November, details of which were "enough to freeze one's blood and excite our wonder that such monsters in human form should be found in existence".

The evidence in such a trial, he said, must establish two points: one, that a murder has been perpetrated and, two, that the prisoners committed the crime. On the first point it was true that the medical evidence was inconclusive, but Mary Docherty was in perfect health at eleven o'clock on Hallowe'en, yet at twelve she was dead. Added to the medical opinion were the facts given by the Hares, and here the Lord Advocate admitted that he had been reluctant to admit them as witnesses.

He digressed to excuse his reliance on the Hares.

I considered a knowledge of these matters indispensable, and as being of infinitely more public importance, than any punishment which could be inflicted on these offenders. I did not think then, nor do I now, that such information was too dearly purchased, by admitting some of these individuals to give evidence . . . Hare accordingly made; and from the information so furnished, the two other crimes stated in the libel, which otherwise would have never been rendered certain, or have made their appearance in a court of law, have been brought to light in such a way as to warrant my preferring them as substantive charges against the prisoners. . . .

It is naturally revolting to see such criminals escape even the punishment of human laws; but this must be borne, in order to avoid greater evils. . . .

I do not present these persons to you as unexceptionable witnesses; Assuredly they are great criminals, but the law has said that their testimony is admissible, and thus pronounced it not undeserving of all credit. It is for you to judge of the degree of credit to which they are entitled.

You saw them examined, and will draw your own conclusions. I may be prejudiced, but to me it did appear that while the evidence of the wife was on many points exceptionable, Hare himself spoke the truth.

The facts from other witnesses tended to confirm the Hares' story, but the Lord Advocate had no reservations about their culpability.

That both Burke and Hare were participants in this foul act, no one can doubt. And I need not state to you that it matters not which was the principal aggressor in its execution. They are both, art and part, guilty of murder.

Nelly, His Lordship maintained, clearly knew of Burke's intention and not only did nothing to prevent the murder but *helped* him by preventing Mary Docherty from leaving when the fight began. Indeed, the real reason for the rush to the passage when the attack began was to stop anyone from entering and to warn of interrupters. Furthermore, Mrs Burke tried to bribe the Grays and she followed the procession to Surgeons' Square to sell the body.

It was nearly three o'clock on Christmas morning, and the trial had lasted seventeen hours as the Lord Advocate ended: "I now conclude the long, anxious and painful duty which I have had to perform from the day when this crime was committed, down to the present hour, by demanding at your hands, in the name of the country, a verdict of guilty against both these prisoners at the bar".

The Dean of the Faculty now turned to the jury. "The great difficulty which you have to encounter in this case," he told them, "is to separate in your minds that which truly is matter of evidence before you from grounds of belief or suspicion received from other sources—from common talk, from newspapers, from handbills industriously circulated. It is a delicate and difficult task."

Burke—and Hare, too—were bodysnatchers, he told the jury, "though William Hare, with his usual adherence to truth, chooses to deny this unquestionable fact". Moncrieff held that the woman had died through intoxication or by accident, in an affray, or perhaps had been killed on a sudden impulse by Hare, and that Burke had agreed to help in disposing of the body for money.

"You may condemn him if you please—you may say he is destitute of common feeling if you like; but the question would be could it be necessarily inferred that he had committed the murder as charged? He is not on trial for procuring subjects for anatomists."

89

And Burke was not the only person whose way of life was open to question. The Hares, The Grays, the Connoways and others in the case drank morning noon and night and they quarrelled constantly until by Hallowe'en there was a complete riot within the walls of the house where Mary Docherty died. In such circumstances there was more than a possibility of death by accident, or death by violence unpremeditated.

The prosecutor's case depended on the alleged accomplices. Without the Hares the court would have little evidence of either crime or criminal; if the Lord Advocate had thought otherwise the Hares would have been alongside Burke at the bar and not in the witness box.

Moncrieff made good use of all the doubts—especially the questions unanswered by the medical evidence—and put forward Burke's invitation to Mary to come to his house for breakfast as an act of kindness. As for his visits to Paterson's house, these were perfectly normal in this trade as a resurrectionist. Moncrieff saved his attack on the Hares to the last. One by one he sought out the inconsistencies in their testimony. "If a man's life, or liberty, or character were to hang on the breath of such witnesses as Hare and his wife what security could any man have for his existence in society for a single hour?"

He had spoken for two hours, and at five o'clock he handed over to Henry Cockburn to sum up on behalf of Nelly McDougal. The trial had now lasted nineteen hours without break and Cockburn must have been exhausted, but he knew that Helen McDougal's life depended on him, and once again he took a warm and human tack which could not be ignored by the most determined member of the jury. Advocates and Writers to the Signet, cramped and happed up in their gowns against the cold, hung on every word. It was with the greatest regret that the *Courant* had to declare its deadline reached and write: "5.30 a.m. We are under the necessity of going to press; but the moment the result is known, we will publish a second edition."

In his opening sentences Cockburn said, "I feel the firmest conviction that you can pronounce no verdict . . . but one that the charge against her has not been proven." After that he hurried to the textbooks to make his points. To all intents and purposes the couple were married, and Helen, as the wife of a resurrectionist, could not have lived without seeing many things which are better imagined than told. As far as Mary Docherty was concerned it had not been asserted that she touched the woman: indeed, it was proved that she fled from the room where the murder took place. Although Nelly denied that it was she who cried, "Murder" and "Police", Cockburn confidently put forward the view that as soon as she saw what was happening Nelly rushed out to give the alarm. Of course she had not betrayed her husband.

It was her misfortune to live in a situation in which, even when there was no idea of anything like murder, she was habitually obliged to make false statements to account for the possession of dead bodies, or to avoid the suspicion of having them ... It may be wrong—but where is the son who would not conceal the guilt of his father? And, of all relations, how can it be expected that the wife, whose interest, as well as her affections, are involved in his, is, merely for the sake of justice, to become the betrayer of her husband?

Like the Dean of the Faculty, but much more colourfully, Cockburn made much of the Hares.

A couple of such witnesses, in point of mere external manner and appearance, never did my eyes behold. Hare was a squalid wretch—on whom the habits of this disgusting trade, want and profligacy seem to have been long operating, in order to produce a monster whose will, as well as his poverty, will consent to the perpetration of the direst crimes. The Lord Advocate's back was to the woman else he would not have professed to have seen nothing revolting in her appearance. I never saw a face in which the lines of profligacy were more distinctly marked. Even the miserable child in her arms, instead of casting one ray of maternal softness into her countenance, seemed at every attack to fire her with intenser anger and impatience; till at last the infant was plainly used merely as an instrument for delaying or evading whatever question it was inconvenient for her to answer.

Cockburn was fired. "It is said," he thundered, "that they are corroborated. Corroborated! These witnesses corroborated! In the first place I do not understand how such witnesses admit of being corroborated . . ." Each time the word cor-rob-rated rolled across his tongue like a drum roll. To the jury it was like a clap of thunder. "The prosecutor talks of their being sworn. What is perjury to a murderer? The breaking of an oath to him who has broken into the bloody house of life!"

In that cold and dark morning his words ran round the softly-lit courtroom like a flitting shadow. "Can it possibly be said that there is not rational doubt in this case? So far from it, that I am perfectly satisfied that if McDougal had been under trial for an ordinary murder, of which the public had taken no particular charge, no prosecutor would have seriously asked for a verdict against her upon this proof."

In his closing words Cockburn returned to the phase with which he had opened. To find a verdict of guilty the jury must have evidence beyond that of the Hares. "If you have such evidence, convict her," he challenged. "If you have not, your safest course is to find that the libel is *not proven*."

Not proven! That verdict in Scottish law which lies between Guilty and Not Guilty, but which appears in many minds closer to guilt than innocence.

The Lord Justice Clerk now summed up. Slowly and ponderously he trailed each piece of evidence before the weary jurymen. It was inconceivable, he said, if Mary Docherty died a natural death, as Burke maintained, that the Hares should swear away the lives of Burke and McDougal.

When he completed his careful review of the evidence he said,

I now leave the case in your hands, satisfied that if you have doubts, reasonable and rational doubts, on the prisoners' guilt, or that of either of them, you are bound to give them the benefit of these doubts, without allowing your own minds to be influenced or carried away by any prejudice or popular clamour that might exist against the prisoners. On the other hand if you are in your consciences satisfied of the guilt of the prisoners you must return a verdict accordingly.

The jurymen rose and shuffled out of the court. It was eight-thirty and the first light of Christmas morning was beginning to show through the windows. Burke and Nelly waited, Burke cool and composed, but Nelly agitated and distressed. Several times he comforted her and told her to look at him while sentence was pronounced.

After fifty minutes the jurymen returned and their foreman, John McFie, stood up and gave their verdict. By a majority they found William Burke *Guilty* of the murder of Mary Docherty: the indictment against Helen McDougal was *Not proven*. Not a muscle of Burke's face moved as he heard the words, and when Nelly dissolved into a flood of tears he whispered to her, "Nelly, you are out of the scrape."

The Lord Advocate felt a sense of relief, for the fact that two members of the jury had wanted to bring a *Not proven* verdict in Burke's case, proved that he would never have secured the conviction without the testimony of Hare. He had bought the life of William Burke at the cost of the freedom of William Hare. At that moment it did not seem to the Lord Advocate that the price had been too high. Others were to disagree with him.

In these days it was the custom for the Justice Clerk to call upon one of his colleagues to propose sentence, and the duty fell to Lord Meadowbank. "I . . . suggest that the prisoner be detained in the Tolbooth of Edinburgh till the 28th January next," said his Lordship, "when he shall suffer death upon the gibbet by the hands of the common executioner, and his body thereafter be given for dissection."

Lord Boyle donned the black cap to pronounce sentence, but in doing so he added a further twist to the macabre story.

I am disposed to agree that your sentence shall be put into execution in the usual way, but accompanied with the statutory attendant of the punishment of the crime of murder, namely that your body should be publicly dissected and anatomised. And I trust that if it is ever customary to preserve skeletons, yours will be preserved in order that posterity may keep in remembrance of your atrocious crimes.

Burke and Nelly were led back to the cells, their Lordships

93

retired, the learned counsel complimented one another, andt he advocates and writers to the signet poured into the grey morning to give the verdict to the crowd which had grown in Parliament Square as word went round that the end of the trial was near.

It was ten o'clock on Christmas morning, and the trial had lasted exactly twenty-four hours—a day without halt for rest or food.

NINE

Crying Vengeance

Each of the four principals in the trial reacted to the verdict in his own way. Burke withdrew into a silent morose world as if occupied with thoughts of eternity. Nelly felt heartbroken and lost at the prospect of being separated for ever from her 'husband': Hare was filled with glee at his escape: Lucky and her child waited in their prison cell, forgotten by all. The people of Edinburgh were consumed with burning rage, coupled with curiosity. All through Christmas Day the newspaper offices were besieged, and extra editions were run off to meet the demand; 8,000 extra newspapers, representing an additional revenue of £240, were printed, and yet people asked for more.

Burke refused to confess until he had talked with a priest, but as it became borne in on him that Hare had not been punished, he began to smoulder. After a period of silence he started to talk to the officers who guarded him. "Hare is the more guilty of the two," he claimed, "because he murdered the first woman and persuaded me to join him. And now he has murdered me, and I will regret to the last hour of my existence that he did not share the same fate."

When an officer remarked in his hearing that he could never wish to see a man forgiven who could murder that poor, harmless, good-natured idiot Daft Jamie, Burke stared intently at him for a long time and said with peculiar emphasis, "My days are numbered —I am soon to die by the hands of man—I have no more to fear, and I can now have no interest in telling a lie, and I declare that I am as innocent of Daft Jamie's blood as you are."

About three o'clock in the afternoon he asked to pray and prayed with great fervour for a few minutes, asking forgiveness for his crime and that Nelly be brought to a full sense of the crimes of which she was guilty and atone by a life of quiet piety and honest industry. He asked the prison officer to read to him from the Bible, and as he listened he said from time to time, "That passage touches keenly on my crimes."

Because hostile crowds lingered in the street no effort was made to move Burke from the cells at Parliament House during Christmas Day, and there he fell into a fitful sleep after nightfall, grinding his teeth noisily and awaking in a frenzy. At two o'clock in the morning he was roused, and taken to the condemned cell at the Calton Jail. "This is a bloody cold place you have brought me till," he said, when he entered the dark, freezing cell. Morning brought little comfort: the cell remained cold, cheerless and dreary, and a diet of coarse bread and water was all he was allowed.

He remained devoted to Nelly and that morning, when he heard a woman crying in one of the cells above his own, he asked if it was Nelly. The warder told him it was, and Burke replied quietly, "Poor thing, she has lost her only earthly provider."

Nelly was kept in jail until the evening of Friday, 26th December, by which time, it was hoped, the first rage of the crowd would be spent. She did not realise just how high feeling was running—how could she, for after all she had been in custody ever since the first report of the murders had hit the town?—so when she was freed that Friday evening she returned to her house at the West Port, and remained there throughout most of Saturday. By evening she felt the need for some whisky, so she went out to buy some. The landlord recognised her and refused to serve her. Soon word that Nelly was back in town spread like one of those great Edinburgh tenement fires. In moments a crowd materialised in the street ready to march in and execute justice where they felt the judge and jury had failed. Fortunately for Nelly, the police reached her before the mob did, and they fought their way with batons to the watch house in the West Port.

The mob surged after her, crying vengeance, and laid siege to the building. While they howled at the front the police dressed

MARY PATERSON or MITCHELL.

DAFT JAMIE.
From an Original Drawing._1829

Nelly in man's clothes and helped her out a back window and down a ladder. When sufficient time had elapsed for her to be well clear of the West Port they told the mob that Nelly was being detained to give evidence against Hare. The crowd was still not satisfied, but it dispersed reluctantly.

Nelly spent the night in another of the police offices at Liberton's Wynd, and on the Sunday morning she was escorted out of the town. She went back to Redding in Stirlingshire, where the story of Ann McDougal's disappearance and suspected murder must have preceded her, for she was no more welcome there than she had been in the West Port. Nelly now fled back to Edinburgh, and on Tuesday, 30th December, she and Constantine knocked on the door of Calton Jail and asked to be allowed to see Burke. The request was refused, but Burke heard that she was there and sent his watch to her, saying, "Poor thing, it is all I have to give her. It will be some use to her and I will not need it."

Nelly wandered off into a world filled with hate, recognised everywhere, always reviled. On the last day of the year the *Edinburgh Weekly Chronicle* reported, "Ever shall we regret that McDougal was not made to pay the penalty of her crime upon the gibbet."

It is believed that Nelly now headed south and that even as far away as Newcastle the police had to rescue her from the mob. Again she found safety in prison for a night and in the morning she was escorted to the Blue Stone which marked the boundary between Northumberland and Durham, and left to wander. The strange fact is that this incident does not appear to have been reported in the principal Newcastle newspapers of the day.

That is the last the world saw of Helen McDougal—or almost the last. She is said to have gone to Australia and died there in 1868, but how or where she spent the intervening forty years is not known. Wherever Nelly McDougal lived she must have known great loneliness for she was greatly devoted to William Burke.

Knox did not escape either, although at this stage the press campaign against him was not as open or as searing as it was to become. *The Caledonian Mercury* called for an enquiry into the methods by which anatomists obtained bodies: "The present

97

impression in the minds of the people, it said, is that one gentle-man stands in the same relation to Burke and Hare that the murders of Banquo did to Macbeth. This impression, we believe, and trust, is ill-founded, but the fact of its existence, which cannot be disputed, should induce him to demand an enquiry and other teachers ought also to demand it in order to vindicate their reputation from the foul suspicions which attach to it in the public mind."

On the morning of Saturday, 27th December, the *Caledonian Mercury* also spoke out against the Lord Advocate who was of the opinion that he was legally barred from prosecuting the Hares because of the promise of immunity he had given. Nelly was free, and rumours spread that Hare was about to be released. Rage welled up again: Hare was the more disagreeable of the two men in the case, and in closes and wynds, down alleys and up stairs it was whispered that not only was Hare the worse of the two, but now he had added Burke to his list of victims. Popular opinion attributed the whole ghoulish plan of the West Port murders to Hare and set Burke down as a mere follower.

Indeed, there was a great deal of sympathy for Burke. Cockburn, in his *Memorials*, says that except that he murdered, Burke was a reasonable man. Other writers have taken great exception to this view, but one can understand what Cockburn meant.

The *Mercury* spoke for many when it reported that day:

The conviction of Burke alone will not satisfy either the law or the country. The unanimous voice of society in regard to Hare is, *Delendus est*; that is to say, if there be evidence to convict him, and we should hope there is. He has been accessory before or after the fact in nearly all of these murders; in the case of poor Jamie he was unquestionably a principal; and his evidence on Wednesday only protects him from being called to account for the murder of Docherty. We trust, therefore, that the Lord Advocate, who has so ably and zealously performed his duty to the country upon this occasion, will bring the "squalid wretch" to trial, and take every other means in his power to have these atrocities probed and sifted to the bottom.

All Edinburgh uttered a pious amen to that, but the mob did not sit back and await developments. It was on the evening following publication of this that they discovered Nelly on her release from jail and hunted her through the town, and then a crowd of youths broke several panes of glass in Dr Knox's house, but escaped before the police could catch them. Perhaps this was just as well, for the people would have been very aggrieved if the stone throwers had been caught and punished.

The trial had revealed little information about the other murders which Burke and Hare were known to have committed, and this ignorance of the truth fanned the flames of anger in the city, where it was believed that thirty to thirty-five men and women had been murdered and sold to the doctors in Surgeons' Square. On Monday, 29th December, the *Courant* gave details of the murders of Mary Paterson and Daft Jamie, the first pieces of real information the public had, and over that weekend curiosity was mingled with anger.

Great crowds thronged both Tanner's Close and the close where Burke's house was located. They took away pieces of wood to make snuff boxes as souvenirs, and one man boasted that he had Burke's hammer, while another said he had Hare's whisky bottle. Although the new tenant of Tanner's Close was glad to turn a little money by showing sightseers round, Alston, who had the keys to Burke's house, refused to make a penny profit from it. At times there were scores of people waiting to go in.

The public appetite for details of the crimes and the criminals was insatiable, and every crumb of gossip was eagerly snapped up and passed on. There were rumours that Burke and Hare were so flushed with the success of their enterprise that they were about to set out in the spring to visit Ireland where bodies could be obtained more easily.

An Edinburgh publisher, Thomas Ireland, was quick to see the commercial advantage of this feeling, and he put on the market a part-work which purported to give "an authentic and faithful history" of Burke and Hare and their crimes in a series of six-penny pamphlets. Ireland's work, which ran to fifteen parts, described the events leading up to and following the trial in journalistic fashion. It was only one of many pamphlets, broad-sheets, poems, songs, and prints which flooded Edinburgh from

99

immediately after the discovery of the murders until well into 1829.

Burke was depicted in comparatively few of these lithographs—perhaps the public felt they had taken their revenge on him already. Hare featured in many, and of course so did Knox.

Lithographs appeared by the dozen: of Daft Jamie and other victims, and all sold well. Poor Knox: his name lent itself too easily to vilification and his conspicuous figure was easily caricatured. "Noxiana" was the title of one series of prints, and the caption of another read "Cropping the Nox-i-ous Plant".

He was also recognisable in a series parodying Shakespeare, with the title "Wretch's Illustrations of Shakespeare", and "Dedicated without permission to a pre-eminent Nocturnal Luminary at present under partial obscuration". Profits from the publication were to go to the relatives of "the late, most innocent, inoffensive, well-known 'Daft Jamie' ".

An illustration of Hare standing beside Knox, wearing a mask, but easily recognisable, parodied a scene from Richard III. The caption read:

KR   Know'st thou not any, whom corrupting Gold
      Would tempt into a close exploit of death?
H   I know a discontented Irishman,
      Whose humble means match not his haughty mind:
      Gold were as good as twenty Orators,
      And will, no doubt, tempt him to do anything.
KR   What is his name?
H   His name, my Lord, is BURKE.
KR   I partly know the man: go, call him hither, HARE.

The authors of "Noxiana" sought their inspiration on a much lower plane than Shakespeare. An illustration of Knox dissecting —or more accurately butchering—a pig bore a caption from *Domestic Cookery*, reading simply: "If you can get them when just killed, this is of great advantage."

A broadsheet entitled *A Timely Hint to Anatomical Practitioners* contained a portrait of Knox with scathing verses, and Knox featured in the rhyme which was sung in every street at the time:

" In Scotland, the Slaughter-house-keeper may pay
His Journeymen Butchers, and thrive on his prey :
The victims are quickly cut up in his shop,
And he pockets the profits, secure from the drop.

In Edina town, where your friend you may meet,
At morning, in health, walking forth in the street ;
And, at evening, decoy'd and depriv'd of his life,
His corpse fresh and warm is laid out for the knife."

A TIMELY HINT

TO

ANATOMICAL PRACTITIONERS,

AND THEIR

Associates—the Resurrectionists.

A NEW SONG—*Tune, Macpherson's Farewell.*

WHAT is our land at last come to?
　Our ancestors would weep,
And say, with many, were they here,
　" Look well before ye leap !"

Ye prowling Resurrectionists
　Of every clime and shore,
Remember Burke, that smoth'ring wretch,
　For he is now no more.

This monster, with his meagre chief,
　In actions mean and low,
Resolv'd to rid the land of all
　That wander'd to and fro.

Two buxom females, with those brutes,
　In this work had their share :—
One party coax'd them to the den,
　The other slew them there.

They with the greatest kindness wiled
　Daft Jamie off the street,
Whose playful manners did delight
　All that he chanced to meet.

With Judas smiles they did betray
　The aged Dougherty ;
Who wander'd long from door to door
　In search of charity.

M'Dougal, Paterson, and more,
　Were by those fiends beguil'd ;
Nor did they shudder to destroy
　The helpless smiling child.

Men, women, children, old and young,
　The sickly and the hale,
Were murder'd, pack'd up, and sent off
　To K——'s human sale.

That man of skill, with subjects warm,
　Was frequently supplied ;
Nor did he question when or how
　The persons brought had died !

If he want subjects let him try
　From France to get them o'er ;
For he can get them, when he will,
　Sent at *Six pounds the score.*

Or let him try some legal means
　His subjects to obtain ;
Nor ever more in word or deed
　Wink at such tricks again.

One of the tribe has met his fate
　On gibbet high and strong ;
And if such pranks are play'd again,
　The rest will swing e'er long !

Written by WAG PHIL.

A Second Edition is published, of the Life and Death of JAMES WILSON, known by the name of DAFT JAMIE.—*Price* THRIP *Pence.*

Up the close and doon the stair,
Ben the hoose w' Burke and Hare,
Burke's the butcher, Hare's the thief,
Knox the boy who buys the beef.

It hard for our generation to gauge the effect of the murders on contemporary Edinburgh, but some indication may be gained from the reaction by members of the community referred to in any of the contemporary pamphlets. When Ireland suggested in his part-work that Mary Paterson and Janet Brown met Burke in William Swanston's public house, Swanston immediately threatened to sue him. Poor Janet had her pride, too. When a print appeared depicting her friend Mary in servant's clothes, she was indignant and denied that either Mary or her mother had been a servant.

If Knox was the person most viciously attacked, Daft Jamie was the most popular figure depicted in the lithographs and literature produced about the murder victims. He was shown alone, and with his friend, Bobby Awl, who later died tragically as a result of a kick from an ass, and was dissected like his friend Jamie.

Jamie's simple riddles were recounted round the doors. Children would ask:

Tho' I black and dirty am,
    An' black as black can be;
There's many a lady that will come
    An' by the haun' take me.

What am I?

Answer: a teapot.

Poems were written about Jamie's death, and one was actually passed off as having been composed by his mother.

ELEGIAC LINES

ON THE

Tragical Murder

OF

POOR DAFT JAMIE.

ATTENDANCE give, whilst I relate
How poor Daft Jamie met his fate;
'Twill make your hair stand on your head,
As I unfold the horrid deed :—

That hellish monster, William Burke,
Like Reynard sneaking on the lurk,
Coyduck'd his prey into his den,
And then the woeful work began :—

" Come, Jamie, drink a glass wi' me,
And I'll gang wi' ye in a wee,
To seek yer mither i' the town—
Come drink, man, drink, an' sit ye down."

" Nae, I'll no' drink wi' ye the nou,
For if I div 'twill mak' me fou;"
" Tush, man, a wee will do ye guid,
'Twill cheer yer heart, an' warm yer bluid."

At last he took the fatal glass,
Not dreaming what would come to pass;
When once he drank, he wanted more—
Till drunk he fell upon the floor.

" Now," said th' assassin, " now we may
Seize on him as our lawful prey."
" Wait, wait," said Hare, " ye stupid ass,
He's yet too strong—let's tak' a glass."

Like some unguarded gem he lies—
The vulture waits to seize its prize;
Nor does he dream he's in its power,
Till it has seized him to devour.

The ruffian dogs,—the hellish pair,—
The villain Burke,—the meagre Hare,—
Impatient were the prize to win,
So to their smothering pranks begin :—

Burke cast himself on Jamie's face,
And clasp'd him in his foul embrace;
But Jamie waking in surprise,
Writhed in an agony to rise.

At last, with nerves unstrung before,
He threw the villain on the floor;
And though alarm'd, and weaken'd too,
He would have soon o'ercome the foe :

But help was near—for it Burke cried,
And soon his friend was at his side;
Hare tripp'd up Jamie's heels, and o'er
He fell, alas! to rise no more!

Now both these blood-hounds him engage,
As hungry tygers fill'd with rage,
Nor did they handle axe or knife,
To take away Daft Jamie's life.

No sooner done, than in a chest
They cramm'd this lately welcom'd guest,
And bore him into Surgeons' Square—
A subject fresh—a victim rare !

And soon he's on the table laid,
Expos'd to the dissecting blade;
But where his members now may lay
Is not for me—or you—to say.

But this I'll say—some thoughts *did* rise :
It fill'd the Students with surprise,
That so short time should intervene
Since Jamie on the streets was seen:

But though his body is destroy'd,
His soul can never be decoy'd
From that celestial state of rest,
Where he, I trust, is with the bless'd.

Written by J. P.

N. B.—There will be published on Monday first, by the same Editor, a LACONIC NARRATIVE of the LIFE and DEATH of POOR JAMIE; to which will be added, a few Anecdotes relative to him, and his old friend BOBY AWL :—PRICE THRIP PENCE. The work will be embellished with a striking Portrait of Jamie.

Published by WILLIE SMITH, No. 3, Bristo Port,
PRICE ONE PENNY.

TEN

Blood—More Blood

Hogmanay 1828—New Year 1829: but it was not a happy new year for Edinburgh. For one thing anger was still running high, and for another fear made men and women reluctant to join in a carousal with any but their most trusted friends, and wary of any offer of drink from a stranger. The authorities, too, feared that the festivities might end in an uncontrollable attack by the mob on Dr Knox or other anatomists and their schools. When new year arrived, however, it was a subdued, uncomfortable affair, without so much as a stone cast at a window in Surgeons' Square.

Burke saw the new year in alone in his cell, with nothing but water to drink a toast to the twenty-seven days and eight hours of life left to him. He was permitted no visitors except the clergy, but this did not stop people from trying to bribe their way into his cell. As much as two guineas was offered to the guards, but every offer was refused, except one of which we shall hear more later.

Burke had lived a Roman Catholic—not a very good one perhaps but of the faith—and he was determined to die one. Father William Reid was a regular visitor, but Burke also received visits from two Presbyterian ministers and listened to them all equally attentively. His attitude ranged from sober piety tinged with repentance to callous levity—perhaps this changing state of mind was a true reflection of his actual character. One day, while one of his clerical visitors sat in his cell, Burke lay on his bed silently contemplating, but suddenly he said: "I think I am entitled to and ought to get that £5 from Dr Knox, which is still unpaid on the body of the woman Docherty."

"Why?" replied the astonished priest. "Dr Knox lost by the transaction as the body was taken from him."

"That was none of my business," said Burke sharply, "I delivered the subject and he ought to have kept it. No, Hare has cleared himself by becoming King's evidence, so he has justly forfeited his share of it." Burke remained lost in thought for a moment then continued: "Since I am to appear before the public I should like to be respectable. I have got a pair of tolerable trousers, but I have not a coat and waistcoat that I can appear in, and if I get that £5 I would buy them".

As the days began to lengthen one of the warders remarked casually on this fact to Burke. "Yes," he replied, "but my day is growing shorter."

After a week in the condemned cell Burke announced that he was ready to make a confession, and so on Saturday, 3rd January 1829, the Sheriff, Procurator Fiscal and assistant Sheriff Clerk went to the condemned cell to hear it. On 22nd January these same legal officials were again called to the jail, accompanied by Father Reid to give what Burke had to say "every degree of authenticity". Burke listened as the original confession was read to him, then confirmed its accuracy, and added a few facts to it. One point which he is alleged to have made on this visit, but which was not recorded in the statement, is that the murders would never have been discovered had Gray not found the body in the straw.

A lawyer named Smith applied to the Lord Advocate for permission to visit Burke to take a statement from him, but this was refused. Even an appeal to the Home Secretary did not gain him access to the condemned cell at the Calton Jail. However, where Smith failed another succeeded, and Burke made a second confession. He soon regretted having made this statement which fell into the hands of the *Courant* on the understanding that it would not be published until three months after his death, and on the eve of his execution he signed a paper authorising Bailie Small to go to the *Courant* office and recover it and take it to the Sheriff.

In this document he said that the original declaration which he had given to the Sheriff was the only one which could be relied upon.

All Scotland wanted to know what the confessions contained, but the authorities sat tight-lipped since they still held William and Margaret Hare and were not sure what to do with them. However, a certain amount of the information which the declarations contained, did leak to the press and for the first time the public was given a tolerably accurate indication of the number of murders and the method employed.

Rage was now transferred from Burke to Hare and Knox. The doctor ignored the crowds who howled continuously around his door, and lectured on as if nothing had happened.

At the beginning it did not seem to occur to Knox that he could be linked criminally with Burke and Hare, but public opinion was aroused to frenzy over the murders. Knox was an anatomist; he had employed Burke and Hare to bring him bodies, and that was enough.

He retained his popularity with his students and never missed a lecture. One day when the noise outside became particularly loud and frightening he paused and looked round his class, "Gentlemen," he said, "you are disquieted by these noises, to which, no doubt you attach a proper meaning. Do not be alarmed. It is my life not yours, they seek. The assailants of our peace may be big in menace, but they are too cowardly in act to confront such a phalanxed body of gentlemen as I see before me. How little I regard these ruffians you may well judge, for, in spite of daily warnings and the destruction of my property I have met you at every hour of lecture during the session; and I am not aware that my efforts to convey instruction have been less clear or less acceptable to you."

But 'ruffians' in the street were not the only enemies Robert Knox had to face in January 1829. A campaign was being waged equally fiercely in the drawing rooms of the New Town. Sir Walter Scott recorded in his journal on 14th January: "I called on Mr Robinson and instructed him to call a meeting of the Council of the Royal Society, as Mr Knox proposed to read an essay on some dissections. A bold proposal truly from one who had so lately the boldness of trading so deep in human flesh. I will oppose the reading in the present circumstances if I should stand alone."

The press was loud in crying for Knox's blood. Anatomists in general were attacked by the *Edinburgh Weekly Chronicle*:

It is lamentable to think that the practice of a science, designed for the preservation of human life, should, through the avidity of any individual to possess subjects, have directly tended to encourage its profuse destruction; that the science should have stooped to a junction with the basest and most unhallowed ruffianism, and derived aid from acts which terribly violate the laws of both God and man. In purchasing the bodies which had come under the fell grip of the Burkes and Hares, there must have been an utter recklessness—a thorough indifference as to causes and consequences, which, in point of criminality, very closely borders upon guilty knowledge. These transactions have cast a stain upon the profession, which, for years to come, the fair fame of those who pursue it—(a fame resting not upon their eminent skill than upon their acknowledged benevolence)—will not or cannot obliterate.

The Caledonian Mercury was more specific and much more outspoken.

With regard to Dr Knox, too much delicacy and reserve have been maintained by a part of the press [it stated]. When the activities in question first transpired, it was stated that Knox conducted himself with the utmost civility towards the police officers who sent to his house in search of the body, when the fact is, he swore at them from his window, and threatened to blow their brains out; and it was only upon their proceeding to force the door of his lecture room, that it was opened by one of the keepers. Further, a number of citizens who have been called 'fellows' by the press, because, acting upon a virtuous feeling, they ventured, illegally we grant, to indulge it, by breaking the windows of that man by whose myrmidons the temple of human life has been so often broken into and despoiled. Great pains, too, have been taken to persuade the public that the doctor was imposed upon by Burke and Hare with regard to the mode in which they acquired their subjects; but mark how a few queries will put down that supposition! Were not the bodies—one of them of a girl, with her hair *en papillote*—both warm and souple, repeatedly received into his lecture room? Did not Burke and Hare exclusively deal with Dr Knox, and must not all their subjects have exhibited nearly the same symptoms in the case of the woman Docherty at once satisfied other medical men that she had been violently bereaved of life? And why did not the constant recurrence of these symptoms, as well as the symptoms themselves, rouse Dr Knox's suspicions?

The mob in the street put it more bluntly. "Kill Knox! Kill Knox!" they cried, and they would have done so had they been given a chance.

The only member of Knox's staff who was called to give evidence at the trial was David Paterson, and far from bringing him glory it made him despised by all, including Knox's students and assistants. It revealed that Paterson, instead of being the faithful servant, was in the process of arranging a deal with another anatomy lecturer to sell bodies destined for Knox to him for a higher price. Paterson was sacked, and on 15th January he wrote in exasperation to the *Caledonian Mercury* to assure the people of Edinburgh that he had been "shamefully wronged". He said he had only kept silent on the advice of Dr Knox, who had promised to make it apparent to all that he, Paterson, was innocent.

It had also been most grossly and erroneously reported that I had absconded and been dismissed from Dr Knox's service, [he wrote,] all of which I can prove to be false. My house is well known to the public authorities; I therefore request, nay, even solicit them (if for one moment they conceive me in any way guilty of this late transaction), to bring me to a public trial, and adduce any evidence they think proper, and either let me be found guilty or have the benefit of an honourable acquittal.

The *Mercury* had "a word or two to say to Mr David Paterson", or to be more precise, a question or two to put to him. It asked whether or not he had gone to another anatomy lecturer's rooms at one o'clock on the morning of 1st November, and offered a body of a woman for sale at a price of £15 because Dr Knox would give only £12? And was the body not that of Mary Docherty?

Paterson denied having any connection with the sale of Mary Docherty's body, but he did admit that he had been dealing with another lecturer behind his master's back, and claimed that he had arranged for Merry Andrew Merrilees to obtain a body for this lecturer. By coincidence this body was promised for four o'clock on the morning of Saturday, 1st November. "I confess that the circumstance of the subject coming from the east at the nick of time Docherty was murdered looks rather suspicious," wrote Paterson with superb understatement.

In all probability the story of Merry Andrew's promise to supply a body was true, but in the mood of Edinburgh at that moment, who would have believed it? Poor Paterson: he was badly-paid, yet he had seen the kind of money that was to be made in the resurrection business and had been tempted to try to win some of it for himself. Now he was loathed by all—by the people of the city, by the press, and by Knox's students and assistants.

When this attempt to clear his name failed Paterson produced a pamphlet under the pen name "The Echo of Surgeons' Square". This was a *Letter to The Lord Advocate, Disclosing The Accomplices, Secrets, and Other Facts Relative To The Late Murders; With A Correct Account Of The Manner In Which The Anatomical Schools Are Supplied With Subjects.*

In this 'Letter' Paterson gave details of Burke and Hare's trade with Dr Knox where they were regular visitors and known as John and William. He even claimed that Burke had been a patient of Dr Knox, and came to the lecture room to have his schirrous testicle dressed.

Paterson gave details of his own doubts about the two murders—doubts which were expressed at a rather late date. He made the most of the case of Mary Paterson, which was the only instance in which an enquiry was made as to where the body had come from. On Burke's assertion that he had bought it from friends of the deceased Paterson comments:

It was rather a new thing for me to hear of the relatives selling the corpses of their friends, and I enquired where the relatives lived; at this Burke looked very suspiciously at me and at length said: "If I am to be catechised by you where and how I get subjects I will inform the doctor of it, and if he allows you to do so I will bring no more to him, mind that".

Paterson said he had positive orders from the doctor not to interfere with people who brought bodies to the lecture rooms, so he was "content to be silent".

He now broke that silence to comment that the face of Mary Docherty was a strong livid colour, with traces of blood on the mouth, nose and ears when it was brought to him.

He related how some students had recognised Daft Jamie on the dissecting table, but claimed that Dr Knox insisted that it was not Jamie. It was invariable practice to dissect the oldest body first, but when a panic got up in Edinburgh that Jamie was missing, Knox ordered the body to be dissected immediately, despite the fact that it was the freshest subject in the theatre. Paterson alleged that one of the assistants removed the head at once and that Fergusson removed the feet which were malformed and would have provided an easy means of identification.

All in all Paterson's accusations and allegations smack of vindictiveness against his former employer, and the 'Letter' was clearly intended to whitewash himself at any cost.

Knox's assistants were infuriated at the effrontery of Paterson's 'Letter', and wrote to the *Caledonian Mercury* about it. Paterson, they said, had been presented as the keeper of Dr Knox's museum and as the doctor's assistant, but in fact he was "nothing more than a menial servant, hired by the week at seven shillings and dismissable at pleasure". His duties were to answer the door, clean rooms, light fires, scrub tables, clear up after dissections and to have the dissecting clothes washed for the students—a job which was done by his mother and his sister. The statement further discredited Paterson for being disloyal and alleged that he was on the point of going off to Ireland with Burke where they could procure "a greater supply of subjects and at a less price, the people being poorer there".

Paterson certainly obtained some revenge over his old master, for his outpourings confirmed in many minds the fact that Knox knew more than he was inclined to admit to. The same might have been said of David Paterson.

ELEVEN

The Last of Lucky

The Paterson episode stirred up a great deal of mud. If the public had not been certain about the dubious activities of the anatomists before, they now knew what a disreputable business it was. And they were more sure than ever that they were right about Dr Knox. He was loathed as much as Hare, who still sat in his cell awaiting a decision on his fate, his joy now turned to such alarm that when officials visited him he hid under the blankets and refused to come out.

Hare's continued incarceration did little to comfort Burke, who raged at the thought of his confederate's escape, and the press was equally annoyed. The *New Scots Magazine* stormed:

> We have heard with unspeakable surprise that these judicial investigations are to proceed no further, and that only the miserable wretch Burke is to be yielded up to public justice. We cannot believe this rumour—for assuredly the public mind cannot be quieted by such an imperfect enquiry as this trial had afforded. The Lord Advocate pledged himself to probe these assassinations to the bottom—and to pursue those measures which are necessary to tranquillise the public agitation —a feeling which we are sure at this moment pervades every family, and every mind in the city—and wherever the tragical tidings have been heard. To stop short now, will just be to leave in every breast that undefined and gloomy apprehension which haunts the imagination, and oppresses it more heavily than full knowledge of the real extent of such evils in society— and we have such confidence in the sound discretion of the Lord Advocate, that we cannot imagine he will leave the nest of

monsters, who have taken up their abode and practised the trade of murder among us, unkennelled, and without bringing every individual implicated to a public trial—and disclosing to the community the dangers they have to guard themselves against from such a system of terror and such a horde of miscreants.

The press itself became embroiled in a battle over the Lord Advocate's position, and one newspaper abused another over the attitude it had taken up. There was much quoting of legal precedents but when the *Edinburgh Weekly Advertiser* tried to explain the Lord Advocate's decision, it was attacked by the *Caledonian Mercury* which reported a suggestion that Daft Jamie's mother ought to raise a private prosecution and that a subscription should be raised to enable her to do so. "The promise," said the newspaper, "may be good against his Lordship himself; but it is utterly monstrous to pretend that it can in any way affect the rights of any private party who comes forward to prosecute."

In spite of all the anger of press and public, and pressure put on the Lord Advocate from every side, he still refused to prosecute Hare. On the other hand he made no move to free him either.

The idea of raising a subscription to enable Daft Jamie's mother and sister to institute a private prosecution was taken up eagerly. There were many people willing to contribute towards any scheme which would put Hare's neck in a noose, so sufficient money was quickly subscribed to enable Francis Jeffrey and George Munro to be briefed.

Janet Wilson and her daughter made no effort to prosecute Margaret Hare. William was the one they were after, so there was no point in wasting time or resources on Lucky. On Monday, 19th January the door of the Calton Jail was opened and she felt the biting winds of Edinburgh against her face once more—the first time for two and a half months. From the prison she picked her way across the Bridges through the snow, carrying her baby in her arms, but it was inevitable that someone would recognise her. Soon the cry went up: "Lucky Hare! Lucky Hare!" and the handful of passers-by multiplied into a mob who pelted her mercilessly with snowballs, mud and stones.

The police came to her rescue and took her to the lock-up in Liberton's Wynd. When she was able to leave she set out for Glasgow, but once again jail became her sanctuary. The *Glasgow Chronicle* reported on 10th February:

The celebrated Mrs Hare was this afternoon rescued from the hands of an infuriated populace by the Calton Police, and for protection is confined in one of the cells. She had left Edinburgh a fortnight ago with her infant child, and has since been wandering the country *incog*. She states that she has lodged in this neighbourhood four nights with her infant and "her bit duds", without those with whom she lodged knowing who she was, and she was in hopes of quitting the vicinity without detection. For this purpose she remained in her lodgings all day, but occasionally early in the morning or at twilight she ventured the length of the Broomielaw in hopes of find a vessel ready to sail for Ireland; but she had hitherto been disappointed. She went out this morning with the same object, and when returning a woman, who, she says, was drunk, recognised her in Clyde Street and repeatedly shouted, "Hare's wife! Burke her!" and threw a large stone at her.

A crowd soon gathered, who heaped every indignity upon her: and with her infant child she was pursued into Calton, where she experienced very rough treatment when she was rescued by the police. She occasionally burst into tears while deploring her unhappy situation, which she ascribed to Hare's utter profligacy, and said all she wished was to get across the channel, and end her days in some remote spot in her own country in retirement and penitence.

The authorities, before releasing her, will probably make arrangements for procuring her a passage to Ireland. An immense crowd surrounded the Calton police office this afternoon in expectation of seeing the unhappy woman depart.

The Edinburgh Evening Courant took up the story four days later:

Hare's wife was sent down from Glasgow to Greenock for the purpose of taking passage to Derry in the steamboat for that port, which is no great distance from her native place. In consequence, however, of the want of a bundle of clothes which she could not get away with her from being intercepted by the crowd, she was detained till Thursday, 12th February, about two o'clock, when she sailed in the *Fingail* for Belfast. While in Greenock the police took her under their guardianship, and it was to but a few that she was known to have been in the town till after her departure.

From Greenock Margaret Hare sailed into obscurity. She was never heard of again, although Leighton, in his book *The Court of Cacus*, claims that a woman told him that in 1859 she employed a woman called Mrs Hare as a nursemaid in Paris. Her age tallied with that of Lucky Hare and she had a daughter in her thirties—about right for the whooping infant in the High Court in 1828—and, although Mrs Hare claimed to be Irish, she often sang Scottish songs. If this old nursemaid was indeed Margaret Hare, then she was aptly named Lucky to be so fortunate as to end her days in comfort in Paris thirty years after the West Port scandal.

On 16th January, just before Lucky's release, a petition was presented to the Sheriff by the two Janet Wilsons, Daft Jamie's mother and sister, accusing Hare of the murder of their son and brother. An examination of witnesses was ordered, and Hare at once counter-attacked by petitioning that the warrant be recalled, that he be set at liberty, and that the examination of witnesses be abandoned.

Four days later Munro put the Wilsons' case and Duncan McNeill was heard on behalf of Hare, and the Sheriff gave his decision the following day. He refused Hare's petition but, in view of "the novelty of the case", stopped all proceedings to give Hare an opportunity of taking his plea to the High Court. While the Wilsons' legal representatives were trying to see Burke to take a statement from him, Hare's advisers were preparing to present to the High Court a Bill of Advocation, Suspension and Liberation on Friday, 23rd January. At the same time they petitioned the Sheriff to release Hare from close confinement and allow him to see his counsel, and this was granted.

On Monday morning, 26th January, counsel for both sides put their case to the Lord Justice Clerk, Lord Boyle, and to the distinguished array of Law Lords who sat in support of him—Lords

Gillies, Pitmilly, Meadowbank, Mackenzie and Alloway. Once again the whole story was repeated by both sides and, but for the intense public interest, it must have begun to bore their lordships who had already heard it several times over.

Sir William Rae, the Lord Advocate, outlined the events leading up to the trial. In giving his assurance of immunity to Hare the Lord Advocate did not have one murder in mind any more than another: it was intended to cover all cases that might arise. "In its nature," Rae explained, "this assurance was thus of an un-qualified description and was calculated to lead the party to believe that the possibility of future trial or punishment was thereby entirely excluded. The assurance was so meant to be understood."

In the light of this Rae considered that he was legally barred from prosecuting Hare and to do so would be "dishonourable in itself, unworthy of his office, and highly injurious to the administration of justice".

Duncan McNeill put forward four main points. First in Scots law an associate in a crime who had been examined as a witness in a trial at the instance of the public prosecutor, and answered the questions put to him, cannot himself be tried for the offence on which he has given testimony. Secondly this state of the law was not the result of ancient usage, nor was it due to any statutory enactment. Thirdly, such protection extended only to witnesses called by the public prosecutor, and fourthly the law of England gave no such absolute protection but only a claim to a royal pardon.

McNeill argued that the public prosecutor alone had the right to prosecute, and in Hare's case the public prosecutor had chosen to relinquish the claim of the community against one man in order to be sure of catching another.

Hare had fulfilled his part of the bargain, and the Lord Justice Clerk and the two Law Lords who sat with him at Burke's trial had made it clear that they supported this view. That was the law on 25th December last. If the representatives of the law had erred then, let any change in the law now apply to future cases only. "To do otherwise would be productive of no good object. The ends of justice would not be thereby promoted. The public faith would be broken and, above all, the informant could not have a fair trial."

On behalf of the Wilson women Ernest Douglas Sandford contended that the public prosecutor could not control the right of a private party to prosecute, and the associate in crime was only protected in regard to the particular crime on which he gave evidence. Since Burke had been tried on only one of the three indictments against him, Hare was not protected against prosecution on the charge of murdering Daft Jamie.

Furthermore, at the trial he was clearly warned that he was not bound to answer questions concerning any other murder because he was not protected by the court. And he chose not to answer any questions about the death of Daft Jamie Wilson.

Sandford therefore submitted that Hare's bill of suspension should be refused.

Their lordships did not give an immediate decision: they needed time to pick a path through the legal bog into which the Lord Advocate's deal with Hare and the public's determination to obtain justice had led them. They set the date for the announcement of their decision as 2nd February. In the intervening days the Edinburgh populace was too fully occupied with the execution of William Burke to worry overmuch about justice and William Hare.

TWELVE

The End of His Capers

Burke became enraged every time he thought of Hare's escape. The one consolation left to him on his way to the gallows was the fact that his former confederate was still in jail, and might yet follow him to the short drop at the head of Liberton's Wynd. However, if he hoped that his own execution might be postponed to enable him to give evidence against Hare he was mistaken—at four o'clock on the morning of Tuesday, 27th January, he was taken from the condemned cell to the police station at Liberton's Wynd.

The execution was still more than twenty-four hours away, but the Edinburgh mob was showing such interest in it that the authorities transferred him secretly to a police station just a short walk from where the gallows was to be set up in the High Street close by St Giles at the spot where the County Buildings now stand.

For days before there had been notices in houses, as high as the sixth or seventh floors, offering 'Windows to Let' for the morning of Wednesday, 28th February. Every place was quickly taken up, for people were prepared to pay as much as thirty shillings for a window which afforded a good view of the scaffold.

Soon after midday on the day preceding the execution the area where the gallows was to be set was staked out: strong poles were set at four corners of a square and a chain was looped round these to hold back the spectators. All day the crowd milled around in a "pelting and pitiless storm" watching the carpenters at work. The din of the workmen and clanging of hammers mingled with the shouts of the people when each part was erected. After nightfall torches shed a lurid glare on the black apparatus, and the dark faces of the workmen added to the wildness of the scene. Usually carpenters were so reluctant to put up the gibbet that they had to cast lots to decide who would erect the transverse beam from which the rope was to be slung. On this occasion all volunteered, and put it up with enthusiasm. When the beam was placed in position at midnight three tremendous cheers went up which might have been heard by Burke in his cell.

At two o'clock in the morning the job was finished and crowds blocked closes and stairs as the rain drove them to seek shelter. By five they ignored the rain and began to take up places when thousands of others arrived from all parts of the country around. At six the rain eased, and an hour later it mercifully ceased. Nevertheless, the morning remained bitterly cold and raw.

In the expensively hired windows well dressed ladies and gentlemen took their places soon after, but the common folk had to be content with a rooftop or the street which they packed as far away as the Tron Church to the east and to Castle Hill to the west. By eight o'clock twenty thousand to twenty-five thousand people were assembled—the biggest crowd Edinburgh had ever seen—and they were ready to receive Burke.

Burke was ready, too. He had slept well in his cell on the Tuesday night, and woke a good three hours before his appointment with the hangman. Time hung heavily—"Oh that the hour was come which shall separate me from this world," he said at one point. At half-past five he asked to have the fetters taken off his feet and this was done. "So may all my earthly chains fall," he said as he felt his feet free at last.

An hour later, Father Reid and another priest arrived, and Burke spent half an hour alone with them. He then went into the keeper's room and sat in an armchair in front of the fire while the priest prepared to say more prayers and all the official ancillaries of the public execution gathered. Burke prayed earnestly, and when he was exhorted to "confide in the mercy of God" he sighed heavily. While the prayers were in progress two Presbyterian ministers, who had visited Burke regularly throughout his time in jail, arrived to add the sombre weight of the kirk to the proceedings.

Burke then was taken to another room, but on the way he accidentally met the hangman who stopped him rather unceremoniously. "I am not just ready for you yet," said Burke, continuing on his way. Now Burke showed the first signs of emotion that day as he was handed the 'dead clothes', the black suit which he was to wear on the gallows. The suit had obviously been made for a much larger man and it hung limply on him. He then put on a white scarf, and a pair of boots which appeared to have lain in a damp place and had become mouldy. When he was dressed for the gallows Burke was then given a glass of wine, which he drank with the toast: "Farewell to all present and the rest of my friends."

Williams, the hangman, now pinioned his arms, and for a few minutes Burke talked with the ministers until the magistrates, Bailies Crichton and Small, appeared dressed in their robes of office. Burke solemnly thanked the two bailies for their kindness to him, then he went round his jailers—the Governor, his deputy, and Mr and Mrs Christie who had charge of the prison at Liberton's Wynd—and thanked all of them for their courtesy to him.

It was now eight o'clock and time for the little procession to set out on the short walk to the top of Liberton's Wynd. As Burke walked firmly at the side of Father Reid he probably recalled the last time he had walked up this wynd—on the night of 1st November to fetch a porter to dispose of the body of Mary Docherty when the Grays were threatening to go to the police.

As they emerged in the square, where the gallows stood a tremendous cry went up from the crowd. For the second and last time that day Burke's composure was shaken, and he hurried unsteadily up the steps to the platform as if anxious to finish it all. Pandemonium broke loose: curses and insults were thrown at him, and for a moment he looked defiantly over the spectators. He knelt and prayed with the priests, and the ministers added their prayers, but the mob was now turning the event into a fair. Those who could not see Burke's face shouted for him to be turned towards them, and they would not be silenced even by a signal from the magistrates that Burke was praying. The mob was now in full cry: it wanted vengeance, and Burke alone would not satisfy them. "Hare! Hare!" they cried. "Hang Hare too! Then they remembered Knox. "Hang Knox! Hang Knox!" was added to the shouts. "He's a noxious morsel," interposed a wit. Burke rose from his knees and took his place on the drop. It was just ten past eight. The cries from the street grew louder and coarser. "Murderer," they yelled, "Choke him!" The mob coined a new word at that moment. "Burke him! Burke him!" they screamed. "Burke the bugger; don't waste rope on him!"

They remembered Daft Jamie too, and shouted, "You bastard, you'll see Daft Jamie in a minute." But all the time they returned to the cry of "Hang Hare! Hang Knox!"

On the gallows platform the executioner found difficulty in adjusting the rope and had to untie the handkerchief with which Burke was blindfolded. "The knot's behind," said Burke helpfully; these were the only words he uttered on the scaffold. As this was being done the priest instructed him, "Now say your creed, and when you come to the words 'Lord Jesus Christ' give the signal and die with His blessed name in your mouth."

The hangman stepped forward and pulled a white cotton nightcap over Burke's eyes. Burke prayed, and at a quarter-past eight precisely he dropped the handkerchief which was the signal that he was ready to die. The platform fell away, and William Burke was launched into eternity.

At that moment only one reporter showed a grain of compassion. "In all the vast multitude," he wrote, "there was not manifested one solitary expression of sympathy. No one said, 'God bless him', but each vied with another in showering their exultation by shouting, clapping of hands, and waving of hats."

In one corner of the crowd a cry of "Surgeons' Square" went up, and a group of men set out for there, but the police were prepared for this and drove them off. In another part of the crowd a baker passed through the throng with a board on his head as if to indicate that life in Edinburgh was returning to normal. The magistrates, clergy and executioner had done their work, and now they left the scaffold in charge of half-a-dozen city officials who looked as if they would willingly have followed their superiors.

For five minutes the body hung inert, then the feet made a

slight convulsive motion and another cheer went up. This happened two more times before Burke found eternal escape.

At five to nine the executioner and the bailies reappeared, and the executioner lowered the body to three great cheers from those who still waited in the street. From a seething mob an hour before, the spectators had turned to a good humoured crowd. "Their desires were gratified," said Ireland in his part-work, "their aspirations were answered, the arch-criminal had met with his doom, and there was for the present nothing to ruffle their tempers."

Shavings from the coffin were thrown over the spectators like confetti and immediately there was a rush to cut pieces off the rope to take away as souvenirs. As this was happening the body was carried back to the police office at Liberton's Wynd, and the carpenters began to dismantle the scaffold. By half-past eleven every trace of Burke's execution had vanished, and the crowd went home.

Attention now turned to the University where Dr Monro was to carry out the second part of the sentence. All day the lecture rooms were beset by crowds, but the body was kept at Liberton's Wynd until the early hours of Thursday morning. During that morning all those with enough influence to gain admittance visited Monro's rooms to view the body—Liston the surgeon, George Combe the phrenologist, Sir William Hamilton the philosopher, and Joseph the sculptor who took a bust of Burke.

At one o'clock the public dissection began, accompanied by Monro's lecture. Suddenly Alexander Monro became the most popular anatomy lecturer in Edinburgh with every doctor, student and hanger-on clamouring to hear him. First the scalp was removed to show the muscles of the upper part of the head; then the skull was sawn away to expose the brain. As this was done an enormous quantity of blood gushed out, so that by the end of the lecture at three o'clock the room was like a butcher's shambles with the floor all bloody and trodden upon. What capital Robert Knox might have made out of this butchery!

In the latter stages of the lecture attention was divided equally between Monro and the door of the room for, by half-past two the College was besieged by students who resented the fact that tickets had been given to all who had influence enough to obtain them, while they, the regular students, were kept out. The police were called, but this made the students angrier. They charged the policemen, fighting and smashing windows, and were only driven off by police batons. The Lord Provost and Bailie Small rushed on to the battlefield to mediate, but found the students in no mood for peace. The Lord Provost, a spectator recorded, "was glad to retire with whole bones, amidst the hootings of the obstreperous youth who lavished opprobious epithets on the magistrates . . . who displayed considerable activity and harangued the assemblage from time to time with apparently very little effect".

The battle raged for an hour and a half, with the police so over-matched that almost every time they took a prisoner he was rescued by his fellow students. A few students were put in Monro's rooms and held there until Dr Christison negotiated peace at four o'clock; The authorities agreed to allow the students into the lecture theatre in batches of fifty with Christison personally guaranteeing their good behaviour, and for the rest of the day the students passed through the room to view the bloody mess to which Monro had reduced William Burke.

Friday was 'open' viewing day! From ten in the morning until dusk a long line filed through the College square, up the stair to Monro's lecture room, past the body and out another door. Some hesitated at the entrance, half inclined to go back, but the advancing file pushed them on. Others just smiled, showing no emotion whatever. Among the estimated crowd of twenty-five thousand men were seven women whose presence shocked Edinburgh much more than the sideshow into which the pallid figure on the black marble slab had been turned. The people would have been pleased to continue the viewing for several days, but authorities by now had had enough and those who swarmed round the University on Saturday were turned away disappointed.

Edinburgh did not baulk at turning Burke into a permanent peep show. His skeleton was carefully preserved, and can still be seen in the anatomical museum of Edinburgh University.

Such was the people's vengeance on William Burke.

Sir Walter Scott expressed the view of many thinking men when he wrote in his Journal:

The corpse of the murderer Burke is now lying in state at the College, in the anatomical class, and all the world flock to see him. Who is he that says that we are not ill to please in our objects of curiosity? The strange means by which the wretch made money are scarce more disgusting than the eager curiosity with which the public have licked up all the carrion details of this business.

When the students laid down their weapons the war was taken up by the phrenologists under George Combe and their metaphysical opponents under Sir William Hamilton. This was a pamphlet war rather than one of fisticuffs or batons, but it was fought with equal venom. Phrenology was then at its zenith, and Combe had just begun his series of winter lectures three weeks before to an audience which never fell below one hundred people. Burke's head was now measured and mapped by Combe to show the characteristics of a genuine murderer. There then followed a measuring of craniums such as Edinburgh had never known, but alas, phrenology proved less reliable than its supporters had believed it to be, and many innocent individuals found their aggressiveness, lack of wit and so on matched the characteristics of the most fiendish murder of the day! As one commentator put it: "Even wise people who never had any doubt of the smallness of their destructiveness, were startled into the conviction that they required not only to take care of themselves, but to be taken care of by others."

The war between Combe and Hamilton resulted in a defeat for the phrenologists, but it did keep Edinburgh entertained for a long time.

The pamphleteers also kept up their output. Confessions appeared almost as soon as Burke was cut down from the gallows, and as far away as Newcastle the *Chronicle* reported: "As usual the culprit's last dying speech was hawked about the streets of this town long before any intelligence of his execution could possibly have been received."

The execution lent new impetus to the versifiers who set pen to paper with renewed vigour, but no improvement in talent. An elegy on Burke soon appeared:

Now Willie Burke, he's e'en awa'
    An' ta'en his last adieu.
Nae mair he'll choke or stap the breath,
    O' puir folk when they're fu'.
On subject gear nae mair he'll drink,
    Nae mair he'll laugh or sport;
And throw the whisky on the roof,
    Or feight in the West Port.
Nae mair he'll creep below the bed,
    And sham his magic vapours,
For he's awa' to his lang hame.
    Hare ended a' his capers.

"Hare ended a' his capers": it was an appropriate epitaph for William Burke.

THIRTEEN

"Goodbye, Mr Black . . ."

With Burke executed and anatomised, interest was now concentrated on whether Hare should be brought to trial.

On 2nd February, less than a week after the execution, the High Court met to 'advise' the cause, bringing together the same scintillating group of legal men as had appeared at the earlier hearing.

One by one their lordships gave their decision, explaining the reasons at great length. Only two of them—Lords Gillies and Alloway—wanted Hare sent for trial; all the others upheld the Lord Advocate's opinion. As soon as this decision had been given the Wilson women presented a new petition to the Sheriff, stating that they intended to sue Hare for £500 damages in respect of the murder of Daft Jamie, and asked that he be detained in the meantime.

It was late in the day, but Hare was brought into court and examined. Questions were put one by one, and all the time he maintained silence:

"Were you concerned in the killing of Daft Jamie?"

"Where were you born?"

"Have you any trade in Edinburgh?"

"Where would you go if you were to get out of jail now?"

"Are you afraid the mob will kill you if you get out?"

"Do you mean to go to your native country?"

"Have you any employment in Scotland?"

"What would you do if you remained in Scotland?"

"Have you any property?"

When the first question was put his only reply was that he intended to say nothing more, and thereafter he remained silent except when asked, "Can you write?"

"No, I cannot," he replied.

George Munro, representing the Wilsons, moved for a warrant of commitment until caution could be found. Two witnesses were called: William Lindsay, a fellow prisoner who had known Hare for two months in jail, testified that Hare intended to go to Ireland as soon as he was freed, and John Fisher, a warder at the jail, confirmed this.

Hare suddenly became loquacious, but the confusion of answers he now gave was of little help to anyone. He had no money, so he must find work; he no longer had a home in Edinburgh, so he could not remain there. Perhaps he would go to Ireland, or to England, or he might remain in Scotland. The Sheriff, who was by this time as confused as everyone else in court, thereupon granted a warrant for Hare to be returned to the Tolbooth until he could find £500 as surety.

The Wilsons had won the battle, but they had no hope of final victory, for Hare could never find £500. The position was stalemate, so three days later they withdrew the warrant, and he was free to leave.

At eight o'clock on the evening of Thursday, 5th February, William Hare slipped out of the Calton Jail, and was taken in a carriage to Newington to meet the south-bound mail coach. His jailer, John Fisher, accompanied him, and both were so muffled up that it would be impossible for anyone to recognise them. When the coach arrived Hare climbed on to an outside seat, "Goodbye, Mr Black," called Fisher, "I wish you well home." The coach jerked off into the night with its happed up passenger on the roof. "Mr Black" was well satisfied; he had cheated the hangman, and now he had cheated the Edinburgh mob as well.

At Noblehouse they stopped for supper, by which time 'Mr Black' was frozen to the marrow of every bone. He was glad to get into the inn, but wisely remained in the shadows close to the door, away from the other passengers. After a few minutes someone noticed the shivering character, and asked if he would not like to come nearer to the fire. He was glad to accept the invitation, but as he emerged into the light and thrust his hands towards the warmth, a fellow passenger stopped, stared, and slowly shook his head. That nod, so full of menace, turned the smug 'Mr Black' back into plain despised William Hare the murderer, for his fellow passenger was Douglas Sandford, who had represented the Wilsons in court in their attempts to prosecute him.

Sandford said nothing at the time, and no doubt would have kept the secret of Hare's identity to himself, had Hare not decided to purchase a little comfort and move to a vacant seat inside the coach. Sandford would not have it! He ordered the guard to remove Hare, and as the coach rattled on through the night with Hare restored to his perishing perch on the roof, Sandford told his fellow passengers the reason for his action. At Dumfries in the morning the passengers told their servants who 'Mr Black' really was, and they spread the word to everyone they met. Within minutes news of Hare's arrival was all round the town; the High Street and Buccleuch Street were filled with people struggling to get into the Kings Arms to catch sight of Hare.

At first he was treated well: drinks were set up and toasts were drunk to "Bad luck and bad fortune!" Someone handed him a guinea which reduced him to tears, and Hare soon became intoxicated and admitted his identity, but would say nothing about his crimes. He had done his duty in Edinburgh, he announced pompously, and would say no more.

As the crowd gathered—to eight thousand eventually—its temper changed, and police had to clear the bar room. It was assumed that Hare was bound for Ireland and would take the Portpatrick coach which was due to leave at eleven o'clock. The mob prepared to give him a warmer send off than he perhaps expected, for they decided to intercept the coach at the bridge over the river Nith and throw him into the water.

The two other passengers for Portpatrick were sent on ahead, and the coach left the inn empty. At the bridge a huge and angry crowd waited. They searched the coach and its luggage trunk, but when they found they had been cheated they returned to the inn, angrier than ever, and laid siege to it.

Soon a chaise was driven up to the door, and a trunk was strapped on to it with great show. While the crowd watched this, another chaise slipped up to the back of the inn and Hare jumped out of a window, climbed into it, and was driven off at a great speed.

At that instant the mob realised that it had been duped again, and gave chase as fiercely as the witches of Alloway had pursued Tam O'Shanter's mare. They cut through alleys to outflank the chaise and came within an ace of doing so when the vehicle reached the gates of the jail, and Hare leapt into the building and the doors were banged shut. Within seconds the mob was hammering on the doors, and screaming for Hare's blood.

They kept up the siege all day, and far into the night. Lamps and windows were smashed, and the great knocker was wrenched from the door. The authorities hurriedly swore in a hundred special constables, and armed them with batons to restore order. By the early hours the streets were clear of people at last, so Hare was roused and told to get ready to move. Policemen guided him through the darkened town, and put him on the road to Annan. By dawn he was beyond the reach of the mob.

Rumour and hearsay are almost all we have left of Hare's journey through life from then on. Early on the Monday Dumfries was full of rumours that he had been recognised in Annan on the Sunday and stoned to death, but the north-bound mail coach arrived, and its driver reported having met Hare half a mile north of Carlisle at five-fifteen on Saturday evening. He was warned to keep out of Carlisle because news of his approach had preceded him and an angry mob was on its way to find him. He turned towards Brampton and slept at Tarraby that night. On the morning of Sunday, 8th February he was seen two miles south of Carlisle, and there William Hare vanished.

Of course rumours persisted. One said that fellow workers discovered his identity and threw him into a lime pit as a result of which he was blinded. This story is given some credence by another that a blind beggar who sat on the north side of Oxford Street in London for many years was William Hare. In his book, *Famous Trials of the Century*, J. B. Atlay wrote:

128

Burke the Murderer. "Drawn from life in the Lock-up House on the day before his execution with his consent."

EXECUTION of the notorious WILLIAM BURKE the murderer, who supplied DR KNOX with subjects

It will be within the recollection of many Londoners, who are not yet past middle age, that when their childish walks took them on the north side of Oxford Street, one of the principal attractions consisted in the view of a certain blind beggar, who, with dog and stick, was wont to solicit alms of passers-by. His story was on the lips of every nursemaid, and he was pointed out to awe-struck children as William Hare, one of the actors in the West Port murders.

If this was indeed William Hare, it is a strange ending to his story.

FOURTEEN

The Truth is Out

With Hare released and all hope of any police action ended there was now no reason for the confessions of Burke to be suppressed. Burke made two confessions, the official one which was taken down at his own request before the Sheriff, and supplemented by a further statement on 22nd January. The second confession has a strange history, but very little is known about its origins. An Edinburgh lawyer named Smith applied for permission to visit Burke to take a statement from him and when this was refused he appealed to the Home Secretary, but was still turned away. Nevertheless someone did get into the cell and obtained a confession which fell into the hands of the *Edinburgh Evening Courant*. This confession, known as the Courant Confession, was revised by Burke himself and authenticated by his signature on 21st January.

When Hare was freed the Lord Advocate kept his promise to satisfy public curiosity, and sent the official confession to the Lord Provost for publication. It duly appeared in the Edinburgh newspapers on 7th February.

The Courant Confession did not have such an easy passage into print. On 26th January the newspaper announced that it had the statement in its possession, and would publish it on the day after Burke's execution. As the private prosecution against Hare was pending at that moment his counsel at once applied for an interdict, which was granted. The *Courant* apologised for being unable to keep its promise, but assured readers that it would publish the confession as soon as the law allowed.

When the original interdict expired on Hare's release the *Courant* still could not publish. A new interdict was sought by Smith, who claimed that the document had been intended for him but had been sold to the *Courant* by a warder to whom it had been given for delivery to him. To back his claim Smith produced a statement signed by Burke the night before his execution authorising Smith "to insist upon the delivery of the paper from the *Courant*". This interdict was granted, so the *Courant* still could not print the document in its possession.

Events caught up with the process of litigation, however. The announcement that the official confession was about to be published brought Smith and the *Courant* together, and some agreement was reached so that the ban on publication might be withdrawn. As a result the two confessions appeared simultaneously on 7th February, and the editor of the *Courant* consoled his hurt pride with a claim that the disclosures in his confession were markedly superior to those of the official one.

The claim was fair. The first confession bears all the hallmarks of what is a document taken down before a group of severe legal officials on 3rd January, and seldom goes beyond the bare, bald facts. The *Courant* confession on the other hand, was made nearly three weeks later when death was near and Burke felt bitter against the cunning Hare who appeared likely to be set free. It reads more like an interview with a journalist than a document drawn up in the presence of representatives of the law. The anonymous interviewer (if he was not a journalist) had a journalist's 'nose' for a story and, having found it, he had the ability to draw it out of Burke. In the case of Abigail Simpson, for example, the *Courant* document depicts the whole terrible scene of the poor woman parting with her last coppers to buy drink and Hare's flirting with her as she became more intoxicated. This is a very different version from the official document's statement that "she and Hare became merry". The first confession pursued Dr Knox's relationship with the murderers much more closely, almost as if trying to implicate him in the murders. It states that Knox came in and looked at Abigail's body and approved of its being so fresh, but the *Courant* states simply that the body was taken to Surgeons' Square "when it was convenient", and sold for £10.

The *Courant* document adds considerably to the detail of the murder of Mary Paterson. It includes the pathetic facts that when she died she had twopence halfpenny in her hand which she held fast in death; her body was warm when Burke cut the hair from her head; Knox brought an artist to draw her in death because she was so beautiful. The first confession contains nothing of this.

Perhaps the thing which shows through most clearly in the *Courant* confession is Burke's relationship with his confederates. He did not fail to implicate the Hares as deeply as he could, telling how Mrs Hare decoyed an old woman to the house and drugged her with whisky so that Hare could murder her when he came home for his dinner. He implicated Lucky even more deeply in the murder of Daft Jamie. It was she, Burke claimed, who led Jamie to the house "as a dumb lamb to the slaughter", and it was she who came to Rymer's shop to find Burke and step on his foot as an agreed signal that she and Hare had a victim waiting at Tanner's Close. When the time came for murder Lucky went out of the room, locked the door and passed the key back underneath it. If she played such an important role in this murder why did Burke refuse to pay her the one pound fee which she was always given from the proceeds of the murders for the use of her premises? One must assume that Burke was angry that Lucky had gone free, while Nelly had stood trial. And of course there was also his claim that she had wanted Burke to murder Nelly because she was a Scotswoman and therefore not to be trusted.

Where was Nelly McDougal all this time? Burke does not tell us; indeed, he maintains in his official confession that she and Mrs Hare were in no way concerned in any of the murders, although he believes that they must have suspected latterly that their husbands were in the resurrection trade. The nearest he comes to implicating Nelly is in the *Courant* confession when he says that Mrs Hare and Nelly were not present when the murders were committed, but that "they must have a suspicion of what was doing".

The two confessions are remarkably similar. They agree on

the number of murders, although the dates on which these were committed and the order in which they took place, varies greatly. Even so, this was the first time the public had been told the exact number of the murders and the methods of the murderers.

The official confession gives the date of the murderers' first meeting as about Hallowe'en 1827, "when he and Helen McDougal met Hare's wife with whom he was previously acquainted".

Burke relates: "They had a dram and he mentioned he had an intention to go to the west country to endeavour to get employment as a cobbler, but Hare's wife suggested that they had a small room in their house, which might suit him and McDougal."

Burke gave pensioner Donald's death as the start of the slide into a life of murder, and dated this as about Christmas, 1827. Donald was not murdered; he died and Burke and Hare sold his body to Dr Knox. It was this sale that gave them the idea of murder for profit, and the sixteen murders to which they confessed then followed:

1 "A woman from Gilmerton": spring, 1828 (Abigail Simpson)
2 Joseph the miller
3 An old woman: May 1828
4 An Englishman: soon afterwards
5 An old woman named Haldane: shortly after this
6 A cinder woman: soon afterwards
7 and 8 A woman "with her son or grandson"
9 A woman Burke brought to the house
10 A woman murdered by Hare alone
11 Margaret Haldane: about this time
12 "The girl Paterson": April 1828
13 A washerwoman: September or October 1828
14 "A woman named McDougal", who was a distant relation of Helen McDougal's first husband: soon afterwards
15 Daft Jamie
16 "The old woman Docherty"

On 23rd January Burke added a few details; He confirmed that he knew no more about the victims than he had already told the authorities, and he added that he had not been involved in any other murders. So far as he knew Hare had not participated in any others either, but to set minds at rest he added, "If any persons have disappeared anywhere in Scotland, England or Ireland, he knows nothing whatever about it, and never heard of such a thing till he was apprehended."

As time passed tales going round Edinburgh had become more ghoulish, and Burke felt it necessary to explain that he kept no knives in his house other than ordinary table knives, the knife he used as a shoemaker, or a small pocket knife, and he had not used any of these on his victims. He denied that either he or Hare had been, as was claimed by counsel at the trial, resurrectionists. He also cleared Dr Knox to the best of his ability, by stating that the doctor did not know where he or Hare lived, although Paterson knew.

The *Courant* confession listed the victims:

1 Abigail Simpson: 12th February 1828
2 An Englishman, "a native of Cheshire"
3 An old woman who lodged with Hare
4 Mary Paterson: April 1828
5 and 6 Old woman and dumb boy: June 1828
7 Joseph the miller
8 Woman murdered by Hare alone
9 Cinder gatherer named Effie
10 The woman Burke rescued from policemen
11 Daft Jamie
12 Ann McDougal
13 Mrs Haldane
14 Peggy Haldane
15 Mrs Ostler
16 Mrs Docherty

While the number of murders tallies in the two confessions, the order can be seen to vary greatly. Burke and Hare did not keep records, and those of Dr Knox were never made available to the public, so one cannot say with accuracy the order in which the murders were committed. Indeed, Christopher North's suggestion is as good as any:

First ae drunk auld wife, and then another drunk auld wife and then a third drunk auld wife, and then a drunk auld sick man or twa . . .

There is no reason to believe that the first four victims named in the official confession are not correct, although Joseph the miller seems the most likely victim to have launched the career of murder since he was not enticed into the house, and this death does not follow the exact pattern of the others. Joseph was not a healthy man lured into the house and plied with drink, but was dying and had to be disposed of because he presented a threat to Hare's lodging house trade. Death was near for the miller, and it was a single, simple step from the case of old Donald to help Joseph on his way. Indeed, Burke and Hare would scarcely consider it murder at all.

Abigail's death was given as February 1828 in the *Courant* confession, so she was probably the second victim, and her death was followed by that of the old Englishman who—like Joseph— was sick anyway. The murder of another old woman, whose name is not known, brings us to April, and to Mary Paterson, one of the few victims whose death can be fixed accurately for two reasons —because of her friend Janet's evidence and because it took place the morning after they had spent a night in jail.

Effie, the cinder-gatherer was probably next. In May there followed the murder of another unidentified woman, whom Burke boldly rescued from two policemen who were taking her to jail, her murder brought the year of murder up to June, and the double murder of the old woman and her deaf mute grandson. Certainly the brutal murder of the boy hung heavily on Burke's conscience, and it would explain the reason for the holiday which he and Nelly took in Stirlingshire at that time.

While Burke was away, Hare tried to work independently and succeeded in disposing of one body, but of course this led to the quarrel which resulted in Burke and Nelly walking out of Tanner's Close. Mrs Ostler's death must have been engineered soon after this, because it took place after Burke moved into the Brogans' house but before Brogan decamped with the rent money. Ann

McDougal, no doubt came to visit them shortly after their holiday as a result of their invitation, so her murder was probably the next one.

Burke names Mrs Haldane fifth and her daughter eleventh in his official confession, but they come thirteenth and fourteenth in the *Courant* confession. It seems unlikely that these two murders would be separated in time, and the *Courant* version is probably the more reliable in this case.

This brings us to October and to the last two murders, Daft Jamie and Mary Docherty, the first at the beginning of the month and the second at Hallowe'en.

It is a pity that Hare's confession has never been found to compare it with those of Burke, but it has vanished completely. It was seen by a number of people, however, among them Sir Walter Scott, who confirmed that he gave substantially the same account as Burke of the number and description of the victims, but differed in the order in which the crimes were perpetrated. Hare confirmed that Joseph the miller was the second body sold and the first to be murdered, which is indeed the more logical sequence.

Argument over the order of the crimes hardly seems relevant to us today, and it was no more so to the people of Edinburgh when they read the confessions on 7th February 1829. It was the number that came as the most staggering blow to the community: although rumour had raised the number of victims to over thirty in the early days after the trial, sixteen still seemed an enormous number of people to vanish without question in a twelvemonth. The method was foolproof and but for the curiosity of the Grays, the crimes might never have been detected.

Publication of the true facts therefore proved little comfort to the people of Edinburgh, and it certainly did not pacify them in the least.

FIFTEEN

Sentenced for Life

Publication of the confessions rekindled the smouldering fires of rage in Edinburgh. Anger went far beyond the Scottish capital too—we are told it followed Nelly to Newcastle, Lucky to Glasgow, and Hare to Dumfries and Carlisle. Innocent people suffered when they were mistaken for the West Port murderers. A poor musician was badly injured by village people in Kirkliston who believed him to be Hare, and a woman was attacked in Lanark because she was recognised as Nelly.

In Edinburgh there was only one person left on whom the mob could turn its anger—Robert Knox. Through all the storm Knox lectured on normally and refused to be drawn on the subject of the murders. Friends eventually convinced him that he should clear his name—the necessity of which became more obvious when Burke was out of the way and Hare was free. Without consulting Knox a group of friends set up an enquiry, and this provided material which legal counsel considered gave Knox grounds for taking his enemies to court. He refused because he considered that "the most innocent proceedings even in the best conducted dissecting-room must always shock the public and be hurtful to science".

His friends then suggested that instead of going to law a committee should be set up to investigate and report on Knox's role in the West Port murders. The setting up of such a committee could not be kept secret, and of course it was soon reported in the press. *The Scotsman* announced its formation on 11th February and, despite an assurance that the committee would be impartial, there were many who did not believe that it could be.

The press referred to it as a gathering of Knox's friends, which it certainly was not, although it is true that his enemies refused to serve on it. When Sir Walter Scott was approached he refused "to lend a hand to whitewash this much to be suspected individual".

The Marquis of Queensberry was appointed chairman, but withdrew before the investigation had even begun its work. The others on the committee were John Robinson, Secretary of the Royal Society; M. P. Brown, an advocate; James Russell, Professor of Clinical Surgery at Edinburgh University; J. Shaw Stewart, another advocate; W. P. Allison, Professor of the Theory of Physics; Sir George Ballingall, Professor of Military Surgery; Sir William Hamilton, Professor of Universal History; and Thomas Allan, a banker. Robinson took the chair when Lord Queensberry resigned.

On the night following public announcement of the formation of the committee, Thursday, 12th February, a great crowd gathered on the Calton Hill and marched to Knox's house, carrying a life-size effigy of the doctor, complete with gaudy waistcoat, and labelled, "Knox the associate of the infamous Hare". They marched up the Bridges, gathering supporters and courage on the way, to Newington. Outside Knox's house at No 4 Newington Place they shrieked and yelled, and cried for blood: they hanged the effigy of Knox from a tree and then made a bonfire of it. When it refused to burn they tore it to pieces amidst loud huzzas.

"The aspect of the crowd was very threatening," wrote the *Evening Courant*, "the whole flower plot and railing in front of the doctor's house being literally packed with people, who were shouting in a wrathful manner, blending the names of the West Port murderers with that of the medical gentleman so often alluded to as connected with these horrid transactions."

The police managed to get into the house and held off the besiegers, but a hail of stones was kept up by the mob. Knox put on a great enveloping military cloak and armed himself with sword, pistols, and a Highland dirk, then calmly walked out his

138

back door to the house of a friend. He was not at all overwhelmed by the danger in which he stood, and said—probably quite accurately—"Had I been called upon to defend myself I would have measured a score of the brutes."

Other riots took place that night in the High Street and Canongate. "Another auto-da-fé is meditated; on which occasion the cavalcade will move in the direction of Portobello where, it is supposed, the Doctor burrows at night," the *Weekly Chronicle* warned. "As we have said before the agitation of public feeling will never subside till the city be released of this man's presence, or until his innocence be manifested. In justice to himself, if he is innocent, in justice to the public if he is guilty, he ought to be put upon trial."

The march to Portobello was duly made and this time the doctor's effigy was hanged on the site of the old gibbet.

More then twenty of the rioters were arrested and fined, but the fines were paid out of a fund collected in advance of the riots.

The committee completed its work about the middle of March. On the whole the report was favourable. It found no evidence that Knox or his assistants knew that murder was committed in procuring any of the subjects which he bought. In the light of the information the committee had gathered there were circumstances likely to excite suspicion, but "after much anxious enquiry", the committee found no evidence of these actually having aroused suspicion in the mind of Dr Knox or of his assistants at the time.

No evidence whatever has come before the Committee that any suspicion of murder was expressed to Dr Knox by anyone, whether of his assistants or of his very numerous class (amounting to upwards of four hundred students), or other persons who were in the practice of frequently visiting his rooms, and there are several circumstances in his conduct particularly the complete publicity with which his establishment was managed, and his anxiety to lay each subject before the students as soon as possible after its reception, which seem to the Committee strongly to indicate that he had no suspicion of the atrocious means by which they had been procured.

139

The committee found no evidence of mutilation to try to hide the identity of any of the bodies.

The committee also enquired into the manner in which subjects were received at Knox's anatomy school, and gave as its opinion that Knox had been "incautious" in believing that subjects could be obtained from relatives of deceased persons in the lowest ranks of society. As a result the doctor gave "a ready ear to the plausible stories of Burke", and because he was such a busy man he left much of the negotiation over bodies to his assistants. Like some other anatomists he did not ask many questions of those who were selling him bodies in case he frightened the vendors off.

The committee were especially critical of the fact that Knox's practice did not provide for greater vigilance in dealing with people who offered bodies which had not been interred.

The report concluded:

The extent, therefore, to which (judging from the evidence which they have been able to procure) the Committee think that Dr Knox can be blamed on account of transactions with Burke and Hare is, that by this laxity of the regulations under which bodies were received into his rooms, he unintentionally gave a degree of facility to the disposal of the victims of their crimes, which under better regulations would not have existed, and which is doubtless matter of deep and lasting regret, not only to himself, but to all who have reflected on the importance and are therefore interested in the prosecution of the study of anatomy. But while they point out this circumstance as the only ground of censure which they can discover in the conduct of Dr Knox, it is fair to observe that perhaps the recent disclosures have made it appear reprehensible to many who would not otherwise have adverted to its possible consequence.

For more than a century there has been argument over this report. Some have dismissed it as coming from a group of Knox's friends, despite the fact that Knox claimed he did not know some of the members even by sight. William Roughead, in his book in the Notable British Trials series, uses Scott's word—"whitewash".

In Knox's case, says Roughead, the flaw in the foundation of success was vanity—vanity to stock his dissecting tables at any cost. Of course Knox was vain, even arrogant, but it was not vanity that made him the most popular anatomy lecturer in Edinburgh. Professor Christison made a more accurate assessment, "Knox, a man of undoubted talent but notoriously deficient in principle and in heart, was exactly the person to blind himself against suspicion and fall into blameable carelessness. But it was absurd to charge him with anything worse."

As the committee reached these conclusions Christopher North sat down to pen his piece for *Blackwood's Magazine*. It appeared in the March issue and, despite the committee's report, it reflected accurately opinion in Edinburgh at that moment. North spared no one who had a scrap of compassion for Burke; he gloated sadistically over the fact that the hangman fastened the knot behind Burke's neck to keep him in pain for longer, and he called the *Courant* reporter a "puir senseless driveller" because he deplored the conduct of the mob at the hanging. At that moment, he said, no one but a base, blind brutal beast could declare, "Dr Knox stands free from all suspicion of being accessory to murder."

Dr Knox stands arraigned at the bar of the public, his accuser being Human Nature, [wrote North,] . . . He is ordered to open his mouth and speak or be forever dumb. The interred bodies . . . for the present I sink the word murdered—have been purchased within nine months by him and his, from two brutal wretches who lived by that trade. Let him prove, to the conviction of all reasonable men, that it was impossible he could suspect any evil—that the practice of selling the dead was so general as to be almost universal among the poor of this city—and that he knew it to be so—and then we shall send his vindication abroad on all the winds of heaven . . . If wholly and entirely innocent, he need not fear that he shall be able to establish his innocence. Give me the materials and I will do it for him.

But would he? Was North any more open-minded than the smug Edinburgh establishment—or the rabble in the street for that matter? Would he ever have accepted any reasonable explanation? I doubt it. Even in innocence North was determined to find guilt. "If innocent," North wrote, "he still caused these murders. But for the accursed system he and his assistants acted on, only two or three experimental murders would have been perpetrated."

Knox broke silence only once, to write to the press when the committee's findings were published. Otherwise he continued to lecture and to keep himself as busy as ever—dissecting, studying, writing and looking after his beloved museum. His students remained intensely loyal and expressed their delight in the committee's verdict by presenting him with a gold vase to mark the conclusion of what Roughead calls "the cleansing process".

This presentation brought forth another piece of "Noxiana"— a lithograph of a gold cup bearing engraved likenesses of Burke and Hare, and a murder scene with the legend underneath: "This cup, originating from and as the expression of their high contempt of public feeling, presented to Knox by his enthusiastic pupils." Where the name Knox should have been, there was an easily identifiable likeness of him. The quotation this time was not from Shakespeare but from *Wiseman's Surgery*. "When there is a strong tendency of blood to the head, cupping should be immediately resorted to." After the report was issued and the furore died down Knox tried to continue as before. By the mid-1830s the number of his students began to fall off, and his enemies grew more bitter against him. In 1837 he applied for the chair of Pathology at the University without success, and a little later for the chair of Physiology, but the University would not have him.

He left Surgeons' Square to join the Argyle Square Medical School, but this was not a success, so he toured the country lecturing and writing. He tried to settle in Glasgow, but could not build a life there either, so he left Scotland to live permanently in London.

Knox was poor now: he was unhappy; he could no longer do the work he wanted to; he was parted from his family to whom he was devoted; and still his enemies did not think he had suffered enough. A visit of the Jibbeway Indians to London in 1839, when they were received by the Royal Family, gave Christison a chance to say that Knox ended his life as "lecturer demonstrator, or showman to a travelling party of Ojibbeway Indians". He was struck off the roll of fellows of the Royal Society of Edinburgh, and the Royal College of Surgeons of Edinburgh withdrew his licence to lecture after a great scandal over attendance certificates which a former student had forged. Other lecturers who had been involved, were left free to continue to lecture and the young man concerned was able to practise medicine, but Knox—partly through his own foolishness and partly through vindictiveness on the part of medical colleagues in Edinburgh—was punished for life.

All that was left to him now was to study and to write, among other things a highly popular textbook of anatomy and a book on fishing in Scotland. In 1856 he was almost able to come back into the world from which he had been driven, when he was appointed pathological anatomist to the Cancer Hospital in London. He lived in Hackney, where he built up a small practice and continued to write in addition to his work at the Cancer Hospital. Compared with other ruined men he was fortunate: he had six years left to do this work which, if not his first love, was certainly dear to his heart.

Robert Knox died on 20th December 1862.

In the century since his death Knox has continued to be hounded by enemies. However, few regard him as a monster today, but rather as a brilliant anatomist whose career was ruined by mistakes no more serious than those made by many of his contemporaries. He was unlucky enough to be the one who was caught, but he was also injudicious enough to make enemies when he was on the crest of the wave of success—enemies who were only too eager to hasten his downfall. Robert Knox was brilliant, he was foolish—but he was honest too.

Burke's punishment was swift, sure and complete: so far as we know the other three suffered no more hardship wherever they spent the remainder of their lives than they would have met with in Edinburgh had the murders never been discovered. It is inconceivable that they were ever identified: if they had been, news would have filtered to the press and a hue and cry would have been raised in whatever part of the world they were discovered. One must assume that silence means that they lived and died in peace. If that is so, it was left for poor Knox, the most innocent person in the case, to suffer most and to suffer longest.

North had plenty to say about the West Port murders. Perhaps he should have the last word. His article in *Blackwood's* took the form of a dialogue between himself and various country characters. In that March piece he said, in connection with Nelly McDougal's acquittal, that the jury did what on the whole was perhaps best.

"I doot that," one of his friends replied.

"So do I," said another.

"So perhaps did they; but let her live," North commented.

"Death is one punishment. Life another."

The same might have been said of Robert Knox.

"Noxiana" No. II. The original broadsheet bore the following text:

(at the top)

The Nursery, or Subjects in training for next Lecturing Session at Philadelphia.

"Some men there are love much a gaping Pig"—Shakespeare.

" 'Tis safest taking subjects from the *swinish* multitude"—
                                                                Bacon.

(at the bottom)

The Lecturer, not quite pleased with *his* subject; although a capital one, sui generis.

"If you can get them when just killed, this is of great advantage"—*Domestic Cookery*.

"Brand's Swine bring at present from £5 to £8"—*Weekly Market List*.

',Noxiana" No. IV. The original text ran:

"Gentlemen—I am an older man than any of you, permit me therefore to give you this advice:—never allow yourselves to be too much elevated or depressed by trifles." (Genuine Speech, 12th February 1829)

A real scene, 12th February 1829.

The Newington Auto da Fé, or quite pleased with *their* Subject, although, noxii generis.

> "Quickly and gaily they pulled him on high,
>   From the field of his fame, fresh and gory,
> They served him a line;—he looked vastly shy;—
>   And expir'd in the blase of his glory"!!!
>   Wolfe.

SIXTEEN

Out of Evil . . .

From the moment of the discovery of the West Port murders, Knox hoped that the ensuing scandal would lead to the introduction of legislation to control the conduct of anatomy schools and regulate the supply of bodies to them. Already in 1828, while Burke and Hare were at the height of their career of wholesale murder, there had been much talk about ways of stopping the resurrectionists' trade. Strong views were held on the subject of anatomy generally, and these were not merely expressed by the mob against a twilight fringe of criminals or boisterous students, but against the whole idea of anatomical dissection. On the one side stood those who believed dissection was totally unnecessary; on the other were those who admitted its necessity but who believed it should be practised only on a limited scale.

Many opponents, especially in Scotland, based their objection on religious grounds, maintaining that it was impious to destroy the human body which God had created. Some went even further and claimed that the anatomist's work would cause chaos at the Resurrection as the organs removed by the lecturer and student sought out the rest of the mortal frame to which they belonged. It did not seem to occur to them to wonder where the flesh and organs of those who had died over the centuries since the Creation had gone.

The poet Thomas Hood summed up the incongruity of the situation when he wrote *Mary's Ghost*:

> The cock it crows, I must be gone.
> My William, we must part;

145

And I'll be yours in death, although
Sir Astley* has my heart.

Even those who did not go as far as the religious objectors still
shrank from the anatomist's scalpel, especially if it was directed
towards themselves or their loved ones. The most sensible people
became quite irrational at the thought of dissection or even post
mortem operations on their families or on themselves. In the
House of Commons in 1832, while an Anatomy Bill was being
discussed, a Member of Parliament told how Sir William Myers,
when he fell mortally wounded at Albuera in the Peninsular War
said to the regimental surgeon: "As you know I have always
insisted upon the surgeons of my regiment and of my brigade
having the right to examine the bodies of all the men who died in
quarters and that I frequently attended myself to countenance the
proceeding. I have, I confess it, a prejudice against being opened
of which I am ashamed but which I cannot get the better of.
Promise me that it shall not be done." The surgeon promised and
they shook hands.

A great many people were like Sir William: they drew the line
at the dissection of their kith and kin, but they did not really mind
about the importation of some poor unknown Irishmen raised
from a pauper's grave to provide material for the anatomist in
Edinburgh or Glasgow. They would not dream of going to watch
the spectacle of a dissection, and they would refuse to sit in the
same drawing room as an anatomy student, but they would have
been prepared to close their minds to the ongoings at the anatomy
schools—if only the dead of their own parish were permitted to
rest in peace.

But with the shortage of executed criminals, demand far out-
stripped supply and the sack-'em-up men did a fine trade.

Doctors pleaded for the situation to be regulated. The surgeon
was required to know anatomy and yet he was not given any legal
means of learning the art. Besides he was forced into an association
with the lowest of the low, a position which he hated. The Government itself had two standards: it refused to alter the law to ensure

*Sir Astley Cooper, the eminent surgeon.

an adequate supply of bodies for the teaching of anatomy, yet it demanded that surgeons appointed to the Army or Navy should be skilled in anatomy. This was a powerful argument in favour of some move being made by Parliament, and at last it succeeded in 1828—by ironic coincidence right in the middle of Burke and Hare's year of murder.

A Select Committee was set up with Henry Warburton, MP, as its chairman. to enquire into the question of the teaching of anatomy. There have been many strange parliamentary committees, but this one brought together the oddest set of witnesses ever to grace such an enquiry. They ranged from the most eminent men of the medical profession—men like Sir Astley Cooper, President of the Royal College of Surgeons and the most famous surgeon of his day, to villains who were what Sir Astley called "the lowest dregs of degradation" identified by ciphers and not by their real names.

Sir Astley led the evidence, and his testimony must have made uncomfortable hearing to the committee. "The cause that you gentlemen are now supporting is not our cause, but yours," he told them. "You must employ medical men, whether they be ignorant or informed; but if you have none but ignorant medical men, it is you who suffer from it; and the fact is, that the want of subjects will soon lead to your becoming the unhappy victims of operations founded and performed in ignorance." He told them he would not remain in the room with a man who attempted to perform an operation in surgery, who was unacquainted with anatomy. "He must mangle the living if he has not operated on the dead."

Sir Astley gave painful facts and figures to show how acute the shortage of subjects was at that moment, and he gave as his opinion that this dearth was due to the fact that quarrels between rival gangs of resurrectionists had created such a scandal that it was almost impossible to obtain a body in a London burial ground at all. The men who made up these gangs were "the lowest dregs of degradation; I do not know that I can describe them better; there is no crime they would not commit and, as to myself, if they would imagine that I should make a good subject, they really would not have the smallest scruple, if they could do the thing undiscovered, to make a subject of me". The public at large must have been surprised to learn from Sir Astley that the Home Secretary, Sir Robert Peel, had gone out of his way to avoid prosecuting surgeons or resurrectionists, and they must have been horrified at his arrogant boast: "There is no person, let his situation be what it may, whom, if I were disposed to dissect, I could not obtain." He added significantly: "The law only enhances the price, and does not prevent the exhumation."

Other eminent men followed: men like Sir Benjamin Brodie from St George's Hospital, and William Lawrence and John Abernethy from St Bartholemew's, and they confirmed what Sir Astley had told the committee. Then followed various anatomy school proprietors and lecturers like Richard Grainger and James Richard Bennett, and lastly the resurrection men themselves. No names were given: they were referred to as "A.B." (probably Ben Crouch), "C.D." (probably Joshua Naples), and "E.F.", whose identity is unknown. These three threw some interesting light on the bodysnatchers' trade.

One admitted that to raise subjects regularly required the buying off of gravediggers and sextons with bribes, and this appeared to present little problem. Most were corruptible. Another gave statistics to show the number of bodies he had lifted, and he obviously kept careful records since he said that the figures he quoted were taken "from my book". The witnesses were scornful of the many who called themselves resurrectionists, but who were only occasional operators. "There is a great many of them that profess to get subjects, that I suppose do not get four subjects in a twelvemonth; a great many of them that had lately gone into the business, and have almost been the ruin of it." Worse still were those who posed as bodysnatchers to hide other crimes. They posed as resurrection men just so that they could appear to have a good reason for being out at night with a horse and cart, which they were in fact using for burglary.

The Select Committee revealed to the public at large for the first time the real extent of the resurrection trade, and how despicable it was. It also revealed that the College of Surgeons was not as united as it might have been expected to be. Above all, the report showed that something ought to be done quickly to regulate the teaching of anatomy and to stop the sack-'em-up men.

But, nothing was done. The committee's report was filed away and there the matter rested—until autumn when the Burke and Hare bombshell exploded. At first little could be heard except the strident cries against the practice of anatomy, but sensible men, Robert Knox among them, thought that this case might be just the spur that the Government needed.

Isobel Rae wrote in her biography *Knox the Anatomist*: "Dr Knox hoped that now good would come out of evil, and that the Burke and Hare scandal would force the government to bring this Report out of the pigeon hole where it had been nestling for nearly six months and introduce some effective legislation."

Indeed, in March 1829 Henry Warburton introduced a Bill into Parliament "for preventing the unlawful disinterment of human bodies and for regulating Schools of Anatomy", and in doing so he had the support of the Lord Advocate for Scotland, Sir William Rae, who had been so deeply involved in making the case against Burke and in freeing Hare.

Warburton's Bill was hurriedly got up, and it was not a very good one, but it hardly deserved the debate filled with prejudice and irrelevancy which it met in the House of Commons. Few spoke in favour of the Bill. Some spoke up for the *status quo*, maintaining that surgeons ought to be adequately supplied with bodies of executed criminals, but it was pointed out to them that, whereas in 1733 one person in ten thousand of the population of London and Middlesex had been executed, the rate was now one in seven thousand. Sir J. Yorke offered to augment the executioner's supply with suicides, but he was confronted with statistics to show that Britain had a lower suicide rate than the Continent.

Another Member wanted a ban of two years on anatomy, which he believed, would put the resurrectionists out of business. In the meantime any anatomical research which was necessary could be done on animals. He had the support of another Member who thought a knowledge of anatomy could be picked up, as in the past, on battlefields.

Surgeons had frequently quoted the enlightened attitudes of the Continent to anatomy, and Members now threw back at them the fact that a certain Dr Azoux in Paris had invented a perfect artificial corpse with 1,244 parts, all removable, and which cost only £120. Yet, they thundered, the Astley Coopers still demanded human flesh.

It was proposed that people should have power to assign their own bodies, or those of relatives for dissection, and this threw Members into a frenzy of alarm. One Member told the House: "There are those in great cities who do not scruple to barter the chastity of their daughters. Why therefore should it be supposed that there are none brutal enough to sell the bodies of their own children to the surgeon." Men could not be trusted even with their own bodies. Lord Wynford expressed concern over men "in a moment of excitement or intoxication engaging to sell their bodies to the Jews".

Irrelevancy was heaped upon triviality, and it is hard to decide whether there was not a touch of macabre humour in some of the speeches. When Lord William Lennox wanted to ensure that surgeons or students did not take bodies or parts of bodies home to their lodgings he was told that such a clause in the Bill would be unfair to country doctors who liked to brush up their knowledge from time to time on the subject! And when Members had exhausted the subject of anatomy they turned on the students themselves and their conduct. A Mr Hunt described the conduct of students in dissecting rooms as "too disgusting to describe even in an assembly like this, composed as it is, entirely of men".

Despite all the abuse that was hurled at the subject of anatomy, the Bill passed through the Commons successfully. But on 8th May, Mr B. Cooper, the Member for Gloucester, presented a petition from the Royal College of Surgeons, praying to be heard in opposition to the Bill as they were unhappy about its details. The Bill was at this time generating more nonsense in the House of Lords. The Earl of Harewood raised the matter of the Burke and Hare murders, giving as his opinion that it was a disgrace that these murders had not been investigated more fully, and that the public had not been informed of the result of the investigation.

It was now clear that no one was happy with the Bill and on 5th June it was withdrawn.

For two more years the uneasy situation continued in anatomy schools, for the Government was too busy with the Reform Bill to take much notice of the surgeons' problems. The College continued to fight for the introduction of a new Bill, but nothing was done—until Saturday, 5th November 1831.

Shortly after noon on that day two well-known resurrectionists, John Bishop and James May, called on the porter of the dissecting room at King's College to offer him a subject at a price of 12 guineas. The price was high but May quickly pointed out that "it was very fresh, and was a male subject of almost fourteen years of age". The porter told Bishop and May that he really did not need any subjects at that moment, and he could not pay 12 guineas. However, after some haggling a price of 9 guineas was agreed and the two went away. In the afternoon they returned, accompanied by a colleague, Thomas Williams, and a street porter who carried a large hamper. When the college porter saw the body he thought it had some suspicious-looking marks on its head, and that it did not have the appearance of a subject that had been buried. He asked what the lad had died of, and May, who was now drunk, replied that it was neither his business nor theirs.

The porter told the anatomy demonstrator, a Mr Partridge, of his suspicions and the body was carefully examined by Partridge who found the corpse fresh, eyes bloodshot, jaw swollen, a cut above the left temple, and the limbs rigid in a rather odd position. The demonstrator quietly sent for the police and, to play for time, went to the resurrectionists with a £50 note which he said he must change before he could pay them. May offered to go for change and Bishop said they would take whatever money Partridge had on him and return for the rest on Monday. However, Partridge insisted on getting the note changed, and in this way he managed to delay until the police arrived.

The three men were taken to the police station where another two doctors examined the body, and gave it as their view that the lad had died as a result of violence. There were signs consistent with a blow on the head; coagulated blood was found among the neck muscles, and they believed that death had been due to the pressure of blood on the spinal marrow. When the doctors finished the police began their investigation, and soon they discovered that both Guy's Hospital and Grainger's Anatomical Theatre had refused the body. May, they found, had called on a surgeon-dentist in Newington on the Saturday morning and offered him twelve teeth for a guinea. He told the dentist that they had belonged to a boy of 14 or 15, and it was evident to the dentist that they had been removed from the body with great force.

Soon the police identified the boy as Carlo Ferrari, a poor Italian lad who earned a living tramping the streets with a cage containing two performing white mice slung round his neck. Carlo, Bishop and Williams had all been seen, separately, on the night of Thursday, 3rd November, in the vicinity of Nova Scotia Gardens where Bishop lived. That evening neighbours had heard sounds of a scuffle coming from the house but they had thought it was nothing more than a family quarrel.

How like the Burke and Hare case it was all beginning to look! Now Bishop's home was searched, and two bent chisels, a file and a bradawl, all bearing fresh bloodstains, were found. In the garden bloodstained clothing was unearthed, and neighbours told them that on Saturday, 5th November, they had seen Bishop's sons playing with a cage containing two white mice.

The police now moved on to May's house in Dorset Street, New Kent Road, and there they discovered a bloodstained vest and trousers, the stains on which appeared fresh. This evidence was taken to Bow Street and shown to the three men. May looked at the bradawl and said, "That is the instrument with which I punched the teeth out".

Bishop, Williams and May were brought to trial at the Old Bailey on 1st December. The scene was remarkably similar to that in Edinburgh on Christmas Day, 1828, with a cry for vengeance ringing out equally loudly—so loudly in fact that when a verdict of guilty was brought in the judge had to call for the windows of the court to be closed so that he might be heard passing sentence of death. May had professed innocence throughout and now he turned to the jury and said, "I am a murdered man, gentlemen."

The executions were fixed for 5th December, only four days after the trial, and in the death cell during that time Bishop and Williams made confessions admitting the murder of the boy, and the murder of a woman and another boy earlier. They confirmed that May had nothing to do with the murders, and indeed the evidence against May had not been at all conclusive, so he was reprieved.

The murder method was simple—Bishop and Williams persuaded their victims to drink beer or gin laced with laudanum, and then as they became drugged, the two would lower them head first into a well in Bishop's garden by a rope tied to the victim's feet. It was almost as ingenious a method as that used by the Edinburgh murderers whom they had imitated. On the eve of the execution a crowd began to gather at Newgate, and it grew hourly until there were thirty thousand shouting, screaming men and women around the scaffold in the morning. First Bishop was brought out; then Williams, and as the ropes were placed round their necks the mob became hysterical and rushed towards the scaffold, struggling with police who had to fight to maintain control. Dozens were trampled underfoot, and by half-past seven between twenty and thirty people had already been taken to St Bartholemew's Hospital seriously injured.

A broadside published at the time summed up the end of Bishop and Williams—"Thus died the dreadful Burkers of 1831". And like Burke their bodies were duly passed to the surgeons for dissection.

Less than a week after Bishop and Williams met what every one of the thirty thousand Londoners at Newgate that morning considered their just end, the College of Surgeons presented a new petition to the Home Secretary, Lord Melbourne. This time they wrote: "The large prices which have of late been given for Anatomical Subjects have operated as a premium for murder. If the Council of the College continue to require that those who present themselves for examination shall have studied Practical Anatomy, who can venture to say that crimes similar to those which have just now filled the public with dismay will not be again committed. . . ."

Their petition was hardly necessary. On 15th December, Henry Warburton introduced a new Bill to regulate schools of anatomy, a much better one this time. It laid down that everyone who practised anatomy should have an official licence, and it permitted "any executor or other persons having lawful possession" to give up bodies for dissection forty-eight hours after death, unless the person had expressly stated before he died, that he did not wish to be anatomised. This gave those in charge of work houses and other similar institutions the right to assign unclaimed bodies to the anatomists, and it gave the surgeons access to a large number of subjects without have to rifle graves. Inspectors of anatomy were to be appointed and they had to be given twenty-four hours' notice of the intention to remove a body for dissection. The Bill also laid down that no body could be taken until a proper medical certificate had been signed, and that, within six weeks, a certificate had to be sent to the inspectors, affirming that the body had been "decently interred in consecrated ground".

There was no mention of making it a crime to exhume a body, no mention of taking action against the resurrection men— Warburton was confident that if it were made possible for surgeons to obtain unclaimed bodies from public institutions then the sack-'em-up trade would die. He was to be proved right.

The new Bill had one unexpected clause—it proposed to abolish the practice of dissecting the bodies of executed criminals. The reason was to remove the age-long association between crime and anatomy, and it was one which appealed to the surgeons. Undoubtedly, this in time helped to make the practice of surgery a very respectable one. The Bill had a narrow escape when it came up for its second reading on 17th January 1832, and there was not a quorum present in the House. The Commons was adjourned, and the Bill had to be represented twelve days later. This time it went through smoothly, and on 1st August it received the Royal Assent. Warburton's Bill had become law.

One by one the characters who had disgraced the medical scene vanished, some into respectable jobs, others into poverty, sickness and a pauper's death. Surgery became respectable, and those who had passed through anatomy schools in the days before the Act were left with tales to tell their children and their children's children. For them life became easier and happier: only for Robert Knox did the years that lay ahead bring misery and ill-fortune.

SEVENTEEN

The Drama Ends

The memory of the West Port murders has lingered into our own times, for they have contributed to the language, lore and literature. First of all the murders gave a word to the dictionary—the verb to burke, meaning to smother or kill secretly by strangulation. The word was certainly coined before Burke's death, because, as he mounted the scaffold, the mob screamed "Burke Hare! Burke Knox!" It was taken up by a number of writers including Charles Lamb, Robert Southey, and Charles Dickens who put the word into the mouth of the very respectable Mr Pickwick. Today the verb is seldom used, but it still lurks in the dictionary as furtively as the men who gave rise to it hung around West Port a century and a half ago. It is little used, but it remains ready for use if the occasion should arise.

In legend, too, Burke and Hare are as firmly entrenched as many of the great men of Scotland's history. Most people know a little of their story, but time had blurred the edges of truth, and many think of the two murderers as resurrectionists which any self-respecting resurrectionist would have been quick to point out they were not. For several generations children went in fear of them just as those of earlier generations had been terrified by the Black Douglas. To win perfect obedience Victorian mothers had only to threaten, "Behave, or Burke and Hare will get you."

Children adopted the legend themselves for one of their street rhymes. They would chant:

Burke and Hare
Fell doon the stair
Wi' a body in a box
Gaun to Doctor Knox.

Many authors have been fascinated by the theme
Hare, but not so Sir Walter Scott, who probably felt himself too
close to the murders and their environment for comfort. At the
beginning of April 1829 he received a letter which sent him rushing
to his Journal to record: "I have a letter from one David Paterson,
who was Dr Knox's jackal for bringing murdered bodies, suggest-
ing that I should write on the subject of Burke and Hare and
offering me his invaluable collection of anecdotes." Scott was
scandalised. "Did you ever hear the like? The scoundrel had been
the companion and patron of such atrocious murderers and kid-
nappers and he had the impudence to write to any decent man."
Scott felt himself too decent and as a result he missed the
best collection of real life dramas that could ever have fallen into
any author's lap.

R. S. Surtees was less pompous, and managed to extract some
humour from the scandal when he made Jorrocks confuse Burke,
the murderer, with Edmund Burke, the politician. "Fine speech
of Burke's; monstrous fine speech," said the Duke of Donkeyton
in *Hillingdon Hall*. "He was 'ung for all that," observed Mr
Jorrocks to himself, with a knowing shake of the head.

Thomas De Quincey, too, extracted humour from the West
Port murders when he came to write his second paper on *Murder
as One of the Fine Arts*, which appeared in *Blackwood's Magazine*
of November 1839. *Toad-in-the-Hole*, the gloomy misanthrope
of these papers, who disparaged all modern murders as "vicious
abortions belonging to no authentic school of art", went mad on
the spot when he was brought news of the Burke and Hare murders
and tried to burke the carrier of the message. At a dinner held
subsequently a toast was drunk with enthusiasm to "the sublime
epoch of Burkism and Harism".

De Quincey then launched into a long classical tale of burking
in reverse by a doctor who made a pact with the man who prepared
dead bodies for burial, under which the doctor contracted to

rnish his friend with a constant succession of corpses (burked in his surgery) in return for half of the articles received by the undertaker from friends and relatives of the victims. "The undertaker," added De Quincey, "with equal regard to the sacred rights of friendship, uniformly recommended the doctor . . . in their lives they were lovely; and on the gallows it is to be hoped, they were not divided."

De Quincey extracted every scrap of humour from the joke. "Their names unfortunately are lost; but I conceive they must have been Quintus Burkius and Publius Harius. By the way, gentlemen, has anybody heard lately of Hare? I understand he is comfortably settled in Ireland, considerably to the west, and does a little business now and then; but as he observes with a sigh, only as a retailer—nothing like the fine thriving wholesale concern so carelessly blown up at Edinburgh. 'You see what comes of neglecting business'—is the chief moral which Hare draws from his past experience."

"The toast of the day—Thugdom in all its branches—brought chaos . . .

"The applause was so furious, the music so stormy, and the crashing of glasses so incessant, from the general resolution never again to drink an inferior toast from the same glass, that I am unequal to the task of reporting. Besides which *Toad-in-the-Hole* now became ungovernable. He kept firing pistols in every direction; sent his servant for a blunderbuss, and talked of loading with ball-cartridge. We conceived that his former madness had returned at the mention of Burke and Hare; or that, again weary of life, he had resolved to go off in a general massacre."

Robert Louis Stevenson could not resist choosing Dr Knox's anatomy rooms as the setting for "The Body-Snatcher", a short story which was published in the *Pall Mall Gazette Christmas Extra* of 1884. Although Stevenson used fictitious names for most of the characters—even Mary Paterson was called Jane Galbraith—he did not hide the identity of Robert Knox who was referred to as K—— or Mr K—— throughout. The story gives the impression that it was tossed off quickly, and with little more than half a century separating it from the time of the West Port murders it was—at very least—injudicious to use Dr Knox's name so openly.

James Goodsir, who had been Knox's pupil, was angered by Stevenson's introduction of his old master into this piece of fiction, and he wrote to the newspaper:

> It will be said, of course, that "The Body-Snatcher" is only a piece of fiction. A pleasant piece of fiction, certainly, to attach the stigma of cold-blooded deliberate murder to the name and memory of a man who has relatives and friends and admirers amongst the few still living of his many thousands of pupils . . . When in the guise of fiction an author maligns in the most unmistakable terms the memories of men who have not long departed, he should recollect that some one still may live who can answer and refute his calumnies.

Where Stevenson foundered two others have succeeded in producing compelling drama from the Knox tragedy—James Bridie on the stage and Dylan Thomas for the screen.

Bridie described his play *The Anatomist* as a lamentable comedy, fiction peopled with real and fictional characters, and of course Robert Knox the most real of them all. Unfortunately Knox must be judged guilty to produce drama round him, and Bridie makes Knox aware of the source of his subjects supplied by Burke and Hare as early as the moment when Ferguson recognised the body of Mary Paterson on her arrival at Surgeons' Square.

Dylan Thomas took the question of Knox's guilt further. His purpose was to prove the theme that the end justifies the means. He did that—and more. He declared Knox guilty. The names of the characters were changed—Knox became Dr Rock, his assistant, Mr Murray, and Burke and Hare were Fallon and Brown. Murray discovered the terrible truth of the source of subjects, but respect for his master, his obligations to Knox, and cowardice kept him silent. When Mary Paterson's body was brought in Murray went to Rock and told him that the girl had been murdered.

"Are there any signs of violence upon the body?" asked Rock.

"She was murdered by two paid thugs of yours: Fallon and Brown. I saw her last night after the theatre; she was well and gay. There are no signs of violence upon her body."

159

"Thugs of *mine*, Mr Murray? Do you remember that you your-self paid them for the last *three* subjects."

"She was murdered . . ."

". . . And what if she was murdered, Mr Murray? We are anatomists, not policemen; we are scientists, not moralists. Do I, I, care if every lewd and sottish woman of the streets has her throat slit from ear to ear? She served no purpose in life save the cheapening of physical passion and the petty traffics of her lust. Let her serve her purpose in death."

"You hired Fallon and Brown to murder her as you hired them to murder the others."

"I need bodies. They brought bodies, I pay for what I need. I do not hire murderers . . ."

The Doctor and the Devils elevated the Burke and Hare tragedy to the realm of literature, but the irony of it all is that, although the story was filmed as recently as 1972 Dylan Thomas's fine scenario has never been shot. Instead, as with much of the Burke and Hare literature, even the facts have been abandoned to present the tale in its most lurid and sensational light. This accusation, however, might be levelled with equal truth at most of that which was written about the crimes in 1829.

It is not true to say that Dylan Thomas's scenario has never been performed: it has, and extremely effectively, too. At the Edinburgh International Festival of 1962 *The Doctor and the Devils* was presented as a play on the apron stage of the Assembly Hall, and in some ways this produced an even more effective and more chilling effect than could have been achieved on the screen, for the mob spilled menacingly from the stage like beings returning from the crowded city of 1828 to our own times. Even Dr Rock, in his aloofness, stood out more bleakly alone than he could ever have appeared to his contemporaries.

Throughout the nineteenth century and right up to the out-break of the Second World War the Burke and Hare play was performed by dozens of small travelling companies whose fit-up theatres were known—because the admission charge was one penny—as 'penny gaffs' in Edinburgh and the east of Scotland and as 'penny geggies' in Glasgow and the west.

From generation to generation this Burke and Hare melodrama was a golden magnet, rivalling *Rob Roy*, *East Lynne*, *Jeanie Deans*, *Maria Marten* and *Sweeney Todd*. It was a Saturday night favourite even in such permanent theatres as the People's Palace at the end of Chambers Street in Edinburgh, the Pavilion in Grove Street, Edinburgh, and the old Metropole in Stockwell Street, Glasgow. *Burke and Hare* had the great attraction for actor managers of being easily staged and free of copyright. Indeed, the actor managers had their own scripts or no script at all because the cast played it so often that they knew every line. So did the audiences, and if a new actor forgot his words the audience could prompt him. Equally, if an established actor deviated from the customary words he would be hissed off the stage.

Elliott Williams, a contemporary Scottish actor who describes himself as the last of the barnstormers, played Burke once a week for ten years, and he recalls the days when there were some forty companies touring Scotland with the play in their repertoire. Mr Williams still performs *Burke and Hare* from a script written down in an old school exercise book, but which he rarely needs to consult. His play, based on the traditional script contains snatches of Shakespeare and age-old 'music hall' quips from Daft Jamie, but it has been adapted to suit modern audiences by the addition of songs sung by Daft Jamie and Mary Paterson, jokes about Mrs Hare's relatives in Ireland, a ghost scene and a scene in which an infant is smothered by the vile pair to loud hissings and boos from the audience. Burke was always the chief villain of the old melodrama, with Hare as a comic character who won what little sympathy the audience was prepared to spare for such a pair.

Nowadays, the roles are reversed, and Burke is the weaker character who is led on by the stronger and more sinister Hare. This is how Bridie presented the pair in *The Anatomist*.

Burke and Hare was always adapted to suit the number of actors available—if the company had a second comedy player they would introduce an organ grinder, probably based on Carlo Ferrari, the poor Italian boy who was the victim of the London burkers two years after the Burke and Hare scandal. Some touring companies would even recruit local children from the village in which they were playing to augment the number of victims, and fond parents would flock to cheer with delight as their offspring were 'smothered' by Burke and Hare.

All the actor managers tried their hand at the play—Messrs Rushbury. J. P. Sutherland, L. G. Emberson, Lelend Jones, Arnold Goldsworthy and A. W. B. Kingston. An actor who played the melodrama many times over pronounced Kingston's the best Burke of the early part of the present century. Harry Egan and Ted Monney were outstandingly successful as Daft Jamie.

Robert Lightbody, writing of the Glasgow 'geggies' in 1922, said of Jimmy Canova: "Another of his realistic characters was his Burke in the play of *Burke and Hare*. After his fearful struggle in which he strangles poor Daft Jamie, he coolly took his clay pipe out of his pocket, lifted a lighted candle standing on a table and lit his pipe, remarking in the most offhanded sort of way that 'it was the hardest job he had ever done!' just the same as if he had taken a heavy hod of bricks up to the top of a four-storey building and needed a smoke after his exertions."

Although the heyday of the Burke and Hare play ended with the outbreak of the First World War, the play continued to be seen in various parts of Scotland for many years, presented by companies like Henry Parker's little group, The Kinloch Players, who toured the small towns and villages of eastern Scotland until the mid-1950s. He and his wife Mary Kinloch had formed their company when the Second World War brought about the disbanding of the West Highland Players to which they had belonged during the 1930s. Their company began at Strathtay in September 1941, and from then until 1957 they travelled, with scenery and properties perched on the back of a lorry, all the way from the mining township to the west of Edinburgh to farms of the Black Isle, north of Inverness. Aberdeenshire was a stronghold of the Kinloch Players, who put on six different plays a week in town and village halls.

Burke and Hare was part of their repertoire, and they played it straight, without music or music hall comedy acts. Of course, there was much pure music hall in the jests of Daft Jamie, even in the early literature on the murders. This was maintained in the Kinloch Players' version. A typical example was:

Jamie: Why did Disraeli wear blue braces?
Burke: I don't know: why did Disraeli wear blue braces?
Jamie: To keep his trousers up.

When the audience's laughter subsided the dialogue continued.

Jamie: Why did Gladstone wear red braces?
Burke: I don't *know*: why did Gladstone wear red braces?
Jamie: To keep his trousers from falling down.

All that had changed in the century during which the joke had been made on hundreds of village stages was the tense of the verb 'to do'!

The actors of the fit-up theatre, to give it its proper name which the actors greatly preferred to 'penny geggie', took their work very seriously. Larry Parker, who played Jamie to his father's Burke, recalls Jamie's catchphrase—in response to every threat he would say in a thin, whining voice, "If ye dae, I'll tell my mammy." This always brought a great laugh from the audience, but when the moment came for poor Jamie to be murdered, Burke would turn on him, quite suddenly and snarl:

Jamie, we're goin' to murder ye.
If ye dae, I'll tell my mammy.

This time there was no laugh—only frightened silence.

As in other versions Burke was a vicious, cold-hearted villain. When Mary Paterson had been suffocated Burke would close the scene by turning to Hare: "That was an easy-earned ten pounds— (*pause*)—and ten shillings," and after the great fight against Jamie, he would say, "That was a hard-earned ten pounds— (*pause*)—and ten shillings."

In contrast Hare was a simple fellow, led on by the calculating Burke and hardly aware of all the implications of his actions. As he carried the tea-chest containing Mary's body to Dr Knox's rooms, he would say naively: "Burke, come on, we'll have to hurry, or we'll be late for early mass."

Henry Parker's script, written down in longhand, was borrowed for a production staged in a permanent theatre, the Gaiety in Leith, just after the Second World War. The Scottish comedian, Lex MacLean, played Jamie and, in the opinion of Larry Parker, who knew the role well, it was one of the best performances of the part that he had ever seen.

Burke and Hare was a favourite with Wilson Barrett's audiences when he ran a repertory company in Edinburgh, Glasgow and Aberdeen a generation ago. Even among audiences accustomed to West End plays, the traditional melodrama was called for again and again, and Daft Jamie was one of Wilson Barrett's favourite parts. This was one of the first roles which he played on his return to the theatre after the railway accident in which his back was broken in 1940. Despite the injury, he fought like a demon against his attackers until he was forced up a short flight of steps at the back of the stage, and disappeared behind a curtain where he was to be murdered. There he had concealed a bottle of red fluid to simulate blood, and after the death rattle of Jamie had been heard, a stream of blood would appear underneath the curtain and trickle slowly from step to step towards the audience. As a piece of theatre it never failed!

Alas, it takes more to move audiences today, and in a recent film of the story of Burke and Hare, the little Edinburgh prostitute Mary Paterson was turned into a French girl in a brothel where clients were invited to watch sexual intercourse through spyholes in the bedroom walls.

The *Burke and Hare* melodrama lives no more—apart from Elliott Williams's barnstorming visits to village halls in southern Scotland and northern England. It is still a magnet, if not quite the golden one which it once was, but even Mr Williams admits that it is enjoyed by audiences of farmworkers, miners and their families, largely as a theatrical curiosity. It deserves better, for the Burke and Hare story offers all the ingredients of the theatre— a good basic plot with characters who are theatrical without having to have drama written into them. And always there is the element of doubt about Dr Knox's guilt.

Burke and Hare themselves leave no room for speculation— they were fiends out of hell. Of Nelly and Lucky one can only

164

say that the *Not proven* verdict in the former case and the decision not to proceed with the charges in the latter, is too charitable. But what about Robert Knox?

"Posterity will have to be very clever to judge you justly," a character in *The Anatomist* says to him.

Indeed it will!

APPENDIX

Confessions of Burke

This confession, known as the Official Confession, was made by Burke in the condemned cell on 3rd January 1829, before Mr George Tait, Sheriff-substitute; Mr Archibald Scott, Procurator-fiscal; and Mr Richard J. Moxey, Assistant Sheriff-clerk.

Compeared William Burke, at present under sentence of death in the jail of Edinburgh, states that he never saw Hare till the Hallow-fair before last (November, 1827,) when he and Helen McDougal met Hare's wife, with whom he was previously acquainted, on the street; they had a dram, and he mentioned he had an intention to go to the west country to endeavour to get employment as a cobbler; but Hare's wife suggested that they had a small room in their house which might suit him and McDougal, and that he might follow his trade of a cobbler in Edinburgh; and he went to Hare's house, and continued to live there, and got employment as a cobbler.

An old pensioner, named Donald, lived in the house about Christmas, 1827; he was in bad health, and died a short time before his quarter's pension was due: that he owed Hare £4; and a day or two after the pensioner's death, Hare proposed that his body should be sold to the doctors, and that the declarant should get a share of the price. Declarant said it would be impossible to do it, because the man would be coming in with the coffin immediately; but after the body was put into the coffin and the lid was nailed down, Hare started the lid with a chisel, and he and declarant took out the corpse and concealed it in the bed, and put tanner's bark from behind the house into the coffin, and covered it with a sheet, and nailed down the lid of the coffin, and the coffin was then carried away for interment. That Hare did not appear to have been concerned in any thing of the kind before, and seemed to be at a loss how to get the body disposed of; and he and Hare went in the evening to the yard of the College, and saw a person like a student there, and the declarant asked him if there were any of Dr Monro's men about, because he did not know there was any other way of disposing of a dead body—nor did Hare. The young man asked what they wanted with Dr Monro, and the declarant told him that he had a subject to dispose of, and the young man referred him to Dr Knox, No 10 Surgeons' Square; and they went there, and saw young gentlemen, whom he now knows to be Jones, Miller, and Ferguson, and told them that they had a subject to dispose of, but they did not ask how they had obtained it; and they told the declarant and Hare to come back when it was dark, and that they themselves would find a porter to carry it. Declarant and Hare went home and put the body into a sack, and carried it to Surgeons' Square, and not knowing how to dispose of it, laid it down at the door of the cellar, and went up to the room, where the three young men saw them, and told them to bring up the body to the room, which they did; and they took the body out of the sack, and laid it on the dissecting-table. That the shirt was on the body, but the young men asked no questions as to that; and the declarant and Hare, at their request, took off the shirt, and got £7 10s. Dr Knox came in after the shirt was taken off, and looked at the body, and proposed they should get £7 10s, and authorised Jones to settle with them; and he asked no questions as to how the body had been obtained. Hare got £4 5s. and the declarant got £3 5s. Jones etc. said that they would be glad to see them again when they had any other body to dispose of.

Early last spring, 1828, a woman from Gilmerton came to Hare's house as a nightly lodger,—Hare keeping seven beds for lodgers: That she was a stranger, and she and Hare became merry, and drank together; and next morning she was very ill in consequence of what she had got, and she sent for some drink, and she and Hare drank together, and she became very sick and vomited; and at that time she had not risen from bed, and Hare said that they would try and smother her in order to dispose of her body to the doctors: That she was lying on her back in the bed, and quite insensible from drink, and Hare clapped his hand on her mouth and nose, and the declarant laid himself across her body, in order to prevent her making any disturbance—and she never stirred; and they took her out of bed and undressed her, and put her into a chest; and they mentioned to Dr Knox's young men that they had another subject, and Mr Miller sent a porter to meet them in the evening at the back of the Castle; and declarant and Hare carried the chest till they met the porter, and they accompanied the porter with the chest to Dr Knox's class-room, and Dr Knox came in when they were there; the body was cold and stiff. Dr Knox approved of its being so fresh, but did not ask any questions.

The next man was a man named Joseph, a miller who had been lying badly in the house: That he got some drink from declarant and Hare, but was not tipsy: he was very ill, lying in bed, and could not speak cometimes, and there was a report on that account that there was fever in the house, which made Hare and his wife uneasy in case it should keep away lodgers, and they (declarant and Hare) agreed that they should suffocate him for the same purpose; and the declarant got a small pillow and laid it across Joseph's mouth, and Hare lay across the body to keep down the arms and legs; and he was disposed of in the same manner, to the same persons, and the body was carried by the porter who carried the last body.

In May 1828, as he thinks, an old woman came to the house as a lodger and she was the worse of drink, and she got more drink of her own accord, and she became very drunk, and declarant suffocated her; and Hare was not in the house at the time; and she was disposed of in the same manner.

Soon afterwards an Englishman lodged there for some nights, and was ill of the jaundice: that he was in bed very unwell, and Hare and declarant got above him and held him down, and by holding his mouth suffocated him, and disposed of him in the same manner.

Shortly afterwards an old woman named Haldane, (but he knows nothing farther of her) lodged in the house, and she had got some drink at the time, and got more to intoxicate her, and he and Hare suffocated her, and disposed of her in the same manner.

Soon afterwards a cinder woman came to the house as a lodger, as he believes, and she got drink from Hare and the declarant, and became tipsy, and she was half asleep, and he and Hare suffocated her, and disposed of her in the same manner.

About Midsummer 1828, a woman, with her son or grandson, about twelve years of age, and who seemed to be weak in his mind, came to the house as lodgers; the woman got a dram, and when in bed asleep, he and Hare suffocated her; and the boy was sitting at the fire in the kitchen, and he and Hare took hold of him, and carried him into the room, and suffocated him. They were put into a herring barrel the same night, and carried to Dr Knox's rooms.

That, soon afterwards, the declarant brought a woman to the house as a lodger; and after some days she got drunk, and was disposed of in the same manner: That declarant and Hare generally tried if lodgers would drink, and if they would drink, they were disposed of in that manner.

The declarant then went for a few days to the house of Helen McDougal's father, and when he returned he learned from Hare that he had disposed of a woman in the declarant's absence, in the same manner, in his own house; but the declarant does not know the woman's name, or any farther particulars of the case, or whether any other person was present or knew of it.

That about this time he went to live in Broggan's house, and a woman, named Margaret Haldane, daughter of the woman Haldane before mentioned, and whose sister is married to Clark, a tinsmith in the High Street, came into the house, but the declarant does not remember for what purpose; and she got drink, and was disposed of in the same manner: That Hare was not present, and neither Broggan nor his son knew the least thing about that or any other case of the same kind.

That in April 1828 he fell in with the girl Paterson and her companion in Constantine Burke's house, and thay had breakfast together, and he sent for Hare, and he and Hare disposed of her in the same manner; and Mr Ferguson and a tall lad, who seemed to have known the woman by sight, asked where they had got the body; the declarant said he had purchased it from an old woman at the back of the Canongate. The body was disposed of five or six hours after the girl was killed, and it was cold, but not very stiff, but he does not recollect of any remarks being made about the body being warm.

One day in September or October 1828, a washer-woman had been washing in the house for some time, and he and Hare suffocated her, and disposed of her in the same manner.

Soon afterwards, a woman named McDougal, who was a distant relation of Helen McDougal's first husband, came to Broggan's house to see McDougal; and after she had been coming and going to the house for a few days, she got drunk, and was served in the same way by the declarant and Hare.

That 'Daft Jamie' was then disposed of in the manner mentioned in the indictment, except that Hare was concerned in it. That Hare was lying alongside of Jamie in the bed, and Hare suddenly turned on him, and put his hand on his mouth and nose; and Jamie, who had got drink, but was not drunk, made a terrible resistance, and he and Hare fell from the bed together, Hare still keeping hold of Jamie's mouth and nose; and as they lay on the floor together, declarant lay across Jamie, to prevent him from resisting, and they held him in that state till he was dead, and he was disposed of in the same manner: and Hare took a brass snuff-box and a spoon from Jamie's pocket; and kept the box to himself, and never gave it to the declarant—but he gave him the spoon.

And the last was the old woman Docherty, for whose murder he has been convicted. That she was not put to death in the manner deponed to by Hare on the trial. That during the scuffle between him and Hare, in the course of which he was nearly strangled by Hare, Docherty had crept among the straw, and after the scuffle was over they had some drink, and after that they both went forward to where the woman was lying sleeping, and Hare went forward first, and seized her by the mouth and nose, as on former occasions; and at the same time the declarant lay across her, and she had no opportunity of making any noise; and before she was dead, one or other or them, he does not recollect which, took hold of her by the throat. That while he and Hare were struggling, which was a real scuffle, McDougal opened the door of the apartment, and went into the inner passage and knocked at the door, and called out police and murder, but soon came back; and at the same time Hare's wife called out never to mind, because the declarant and Hare would not hurt one another. That whenever he and Hare rose and went towards the straw where Docherty was lying, McDougal and Hare's wife, who, he thinks, were lying in bed at the time, or, perhaps, were at the fire, immediately rose and left the house, but did not make any noise, so far as he heard, and he was surprised at their going out at that time, because he did not see how they could have any suspicion of what they (the declarant and Hare) intended doing. That he cannot say whether he and Hare would have killed Docherty or not, if the women had remained, because they were so determined to kill the woman, the drink being in their head;—and he has no knowledge or suspicion of Docherty's body having been offered to any person besides Dr Knox; and he does not suspect that Paterson would offer the body to any other person than Dr Knox.

Declares, that suffocation was not suggested to them by any person as a mode of killing, but occurred to Hare on the first occasion before mentioned, and was continued afterwards because it was effectual, and showed no marks; and when they lay across the body at the same time, that was not suggested to them by any person, for they never spoke to any person on such a subject; and it was not done for the purpose of preventing the person from breathing, but was only done for the purpose of keeping down the person's arms and thighs, to prevent the person struggling.

Declares, That with the exception of the body of Docherty, they never took the person by the throat, and they never leapt upon them; and declares that there were no marks of violence on any of the subjects, and they were sufficiently cold to prevent any suspicion on the part of the Doctors; and, at all events, they might be cold and stiff enough before the box was opened up, and he and Hare always told some story of their having purchased the subjects from some relation or other person who had the means of disposing of them, about different parts of the town, and the statements which they made were such as to prevent the Doctors having any suspicions; and no suspicions were expressed by Dr Knox or any of his assistants, and no questions asked tending to show that they had suspicion.

Declares, that McDougal and Hare's wife were no way concerned in any of the murders, and neither of them knew of anything of the kind being intended even in the case of Docherty; and although these two women may latterly have had some suspicion in their own minds that the declarant and Hare were concerned in lifting dead bodies, he does not think they could have any suspicion that he and Hare were concerned in committing murders.

Declares, That none of the subjects which they had procured, as before mentioned, were offered to any other person than Dr Knox's assistants, and he and Hare had very little communication with Dr Knox himself; and declares, that he has not the smallest suspicion of any other person in this, or in any other country, except Hare and himself, being concerned in killing persons and offering their bodies for dissection; and he never knew or heard of such a thing having been done before.

(*Signed*) WM BURKE
G TAIT

On 22nd January 1829, before the same three people, but with a Roman Catholic Priest, the Rev William Reid, present to give the confession "every degree of authenticity", Burke confirmed his earlier confession, and added further details to it.

Compeared William Burke, at present under sentence of death in the gaol of Edinburgh, and his declaration, of date the 3d current, being read over to him, he adheres thereto. Declares further, that he does not know the names and descriptions of any of the persons who were destroyed except as mentioned in his former declaration. Declares that he never was concerned in any other act of the same kind, nor made any attempt or preparation to commit such, and all reports of a contrary tendency, some of which he has heard, are groundless. And he does not know of Hare being concerned in any such, except as mentioned in his former declaration; and he does not know of any persons being murdered for the purpose of dissection by any other persons than himself and Hare, and if any persons have disappeared any where in Scotland, England, or Ireland, he knows nothing whatever about it, and never heard of such a thing till he was apprehended. Declares, that he never had any instrument in his house except a common table knife, or a knife used by him in his trade as a shoe-maker, or a small pocket knife, and he never used any of those instruments, or attempted to do so, on any of the persons who were destroyed. Declares, that neither he nor Hare, so far as he knows, ever were concerned in supplying any subjects for dissec-tion except those before mentioned; and, in particular, never did so by raising dead bodies from the grave. Declares, that they never allowed Dr Knox or any of his assistants, to know exactly where their houses were, but Paterson, Dr Knox's porter or door-keeper, knew. And this he declares to be truth.

(Signed) WM BURKE
G TAIT

THE *COURANT* CONFESSION

This confession, made in the condemned cell on 21st January 1829, was published by the *Edinburgh Evening Courant* on 7th February 1829.
    The words in italics were added by Burke in his own hand-writing.

Abigail Simpson was murdered on the 12 Febaruay 1828, on the forenoon of the day. She resided in Gilmerton, near

Edinburgh; had a daughter living there. She used to sell salt and camstone. She was decoyed in by Hare and his wife on the afternoon of the 11 February, and he gave her some whisky to drink. She had one shilling and sixpence, and a can of kitchen-fee. Hare's wife gave her one shilling and sixpence for it; she drank it all with them. She then said she had a daughter. Hare said he was a single man, and would marry her, and get all the money amongst them.

They then proposed to her to stay all night, which she did, as she was so drunk she could not go home; and in the morning was vomiting. They then gave her some porter and whisky, and made her so drunk that she fell asleep on the bed. Hare then laid hold of her mouth and nose, and prevented her from breathing. Burke held her hands and feet till she was dead. She made very little resistance, and when it was convenient they carried her to Dr Knox's dissecting-rooms in Surgeon Square, and got ten pounds for her. She had on a drab mantle, a white-grounded cotton shawl and blue spots on it. Hare took all her clothes and went out with them; said he was going to put them into the canal. She said she was a pensioner of Sir John Hay's. (Perhaps this should be Sir John Hope).

The next was an Englishman, a native of Cheshire, and a lodger of Hare's. They murdered him in the same manner as the other. He *was* ill with *the* jaundice at the same time. He was very tall; had black hair, brown whiskers, mixed with grey hairs. He used to sell spunks in Edinburgh; was about forty years of age. Did not know his name. *Sold to Dr Knox for £10.*

The next was an old woman who lodged with Hare for one night, but does not know her name. She was murdered in the same manner as above. *Sold to Dr Knox for £10.* The old woman was decoyed into the house by Mrs Hare in the forenoon from the street when Hare was working at the boats at the canal. She gave her whisky, and put her to bed three times.

At last she was so drunk that she fell asleep; and when Hare came home to his dinner, he put part of the bed-tick on her mouth and nose, and when he came home at night she was dead. Burke at this time was mending shoes; and Hare and Burke took the clothes off her, and put her body into a tea-box. Took her to Knox's that night.

The next was Mary Paterson, who was murdered in Burke's brother's house in the Canongate, in the month of April last, by Burke and Hare, in the forenoon. She was put into a tea-box, and carried to Dr Knox's dissecting-rooms in the afternoon of the same day; and got £8 for her body. She had twopence halfpenny, which she held fast in her hand. Declares that the girl Paterson was only four hours dead till she was in Knox's dissecting-rooms; but she was not dissected at that time, for she was three months in whisky before she was dissected. She was warm when Burke cut the hair off her head; and Knox brought a Mr —— a painter, to look at her, she was so handsome a figure, and well shaped in body and limbs. One of the students said she was like a girl he had seen in the Canongate as one pea is like to another. They desired Burke to cut off her hair; one of the students gave a pair of scissors for that purpose.

In June last, an old woman and a dumb boy, her grandson, from Glasgow, came to Hare's, and were both murdered at the *dead* hour of night, when the woman was in bed. Burke and Hare murdered her the same way as they did the others. They took off the bed-clothes and tick, stripped off her clothes, and laid her on the bottom of the bed, and then put on the bed-tick, and bed-clothes on the top of her; and they then came and took *the boy* in their arms and carried him to the room, and murdered him in the same manner, and *laid* him alongside of his grandmother. They lay for the space of an hour; they then put them into a herring barrel. The barrel was perfectly dry; there was no brine in it. They carried them to the stable till next day; they put the barrel into Hare's cart, and Hare's horse was yoked in it; but the horse would not drag the cart one foot past the Meal-market; and they got a porter with a hurley, and put the barrel on it. Hare and the porter went to Surgeon Square with it. Burke went before them, as he was afraid something would happen, as the horse would not draw them. When they came to Dr Knox's dissecting-rooms, Burke carried the barrel in his arms. The students and them had hard work to get them out, being so stiff and cold. They received £16 for them both. Hare was taken in by the horse he bought that refused drawing the corpse to Surgeon Square, and they shot it in the tanyard. He had two large holes in his shoulder stuffed with cotton, and covered over with a piece of another horse's skin to prevent them being discovered.

Joseph, the miller by trade, and a lodger of Hare's. He had once been possessed of a good deal of money. He was connected by marriage with some of the Carron company. Burke and Hare murdered him by pressing a pillow on his mouth and nose till he was dead. He was then carried to Dr Knox's in Surgeon Square. They got £10 for him.

Burke and Helen McDougal were on a visit seeing their friends near Falkirk. This was at the time a procession was made round a stone in that neighbourhood; thinks it was the anniversary of the battle of Bannockburn. When he was away, Hare fell in with a woman drunk in the street at the West Port. He took her into his house and murdered her himself, and sold her to Dr Knox's assistants for £8. When Burke went away he knew Hare was in want of money; his things were all in pawn; but when we came back, found him have plenty of money. Burke asked him if he had been doing any business. He said he had been doing nothing. Burke did not believe him, and went to Dr Knox, who told him that Hare had brought a subject. Hare then confessed what he had done.

A cinder-gatherer; *Burke* thinks her name was Effy. She was in the habit of selling small pieces of leather to him (*as he was a cobbler*), she gathered about the coach-works. He took her into Hare's stable, and gave her whisky to drink till she was drunk; she then lay down among some straw and fell asleep. They then laid a cloth over her. Burke and Hare murdered her as they *did the* others. She was then carried to Dr Knox's, Surgeon Square, and sold for £10.

Andrew Williamson, a policeman, and his neighbour, were dragging a drunk woman to the West Port watch-house. They found her sitting on a stair. Burke said, "Let the woman go to her lodgings." They said they did not know where she lodged. Burke then said he would take her to lodgings. They then gave her to his charge. He then took her to Hare's house. Burke and Hare murdered her that night the same way as they did the others. They carried her to Dr Knox's in Surgeon Square, and got £10.

Burke, being asked, did the policemen know him when they gave him this drunk woman into his charge? He said he had a good character with the police; or if they had known that there were four murderers living in one house they would have visited them oftener.

James Wilson, commonly *called* Daft Jamie. Hare's *wife* brought him in from the street into her house. Burke was at the time getting a dram in Rymer's shop. He saw her take Jamie off the street, bare-headed and bare-footed. After she got him into her house, and left him with Hare, she came to Rymer's shop for a pennyworth of butter, and Burke was standing at the counter. She asked him for a dram; and in drinking it she stamped him on the foot. He knew immediately what she wanted him for, and he then went after her. When in the house, she said, you have come too late, for the drink is all done; and Jamie had the cup in his hand. He had never seen him before to his knowledge. They then proposed to send for another half mutchkin, which they did, and urged him to drink; she took a little with them. They then invited him ben to the little room, and advised him to sit down upon the bed. Hare's wife then went out, and locked the outer door, and put the key below the door. There were none in the room but themselves three. Jamie sat down upon the bed. He then lay down upon the bed, and Hare lay down at his back, his head raised up and resting upon his left hand. Burke was standing at the foreside of the bed. When they had lain there for some time, Hare threw his body on the top of Jamie, pressed his hand on his mouth, and held his nose with his other. Hare and him fell off the bed and struggled. Burke then held his hands and feet. They never quitted their grip till he was dead. He never got up nor cried any. When he was dead, Hare felt his pockets, and took out a brass snuff-box and a copper snuff-spoon. He gave the spoon to Burke, and kept the box to himself. Sometime after, he said he threw the box away in the tan-yard; and the brass-box that was libelled against Burke in the Sheriff's-office was Burke's own box. It was after breakfast Jamie was enticed in, and he was murdered by twelve o'clock in the day. Burke declares that Mrs Hare led poor Jamie in as a dumb lamb to the slaughter, and as a sheep to the shearers; and he was always very anxious making inquiries for his mother, and was told she would be there immediately.

He does not think he drank above one glass of whisky all the time. He was then put into a chest that Hare kept clothes in; and they carried him to Dr Knox's, in Surgeon Square, that afternoon, and got £10 for him. Burke gave Daft Jamie's clothes to his brother's children; they were almost naked; and when he untied the bundle they were like to quarrel about them. The clothes of the other murdered persons were generally destroyed, to prevent detection.

Ann McDougal, a cousin of Helen McDougal's former husband. She was a young woman, and married, and had come on a visit to see them. Hare and Burke gave her whisky till she was drunk, and when in bed and asleep, Burke told Hare that he would have most to do to her, as she being a distant friend, he did not like to begin first on her. Hare murdered her by stopping her breath, and Burke assisted him the same way as the others. One of Dr Knox's assistants, *Paterson*, gave them a fine trunk to put her into. It was in the afternoon when she was done. It was in John Broggan's house; and when Broggan came home from his work he saw the trunk, and made inquiries about it, as he knew they had no trunks there. Burke then gave him two or three drams, as there was always plenty of whisky going at these times, to make him quiet. Hare and Burke then gave him £1 10s. each, as he was back in his rent, for to pay it, and he left Edinburgh a few days after. They then carried her to Surgeon Square as soon as Broggan went out of the house, and got £10 for her. Hare was cautioner for Broggan's rent, being £3, and Hare and Burke gave him that sum. Broggan went off in a few days, and the rent is not paid yet. They gave him the money that he might not come against them for the murder of Ann McDougal, that he saw in the trunk, that was murdered in his house. Hare thought that the rent would fall upon him, and if he could get Burke to pay the half of it, it would be so much the better; and proposed this to Burke, and he agreed to it, as they were glad to get him out of the way. Broggan's wife is a cousin of Burke's. They thought he went to Glasgow, but are not sure.

Mrs Haldane, a stout old woman, who had a daughter transported last summer from the Calton jail for 14 years, and has another daughter married to ——, in the High Street. She was a lodger of Hare's. She went into Hare's stable; the door was left open, and she being drunk, and falling asleep among some straw, Hare and Burke murdered her the same way as they did the others, and kept the body all night in the stable, and took her to Dr Knox's next day. She had but one tooth in her mouth, and that was a very large one in front.

A young woman, a daughter of Mrs Haldane, of the name of Peggy Haldane, was drunk, and sleeping in Broggan's house, was murdered by Burke himself, in the forenoon. Hare had no hand in it. She was taken to Dr. Knox's in the afternoon in a tea-box, and £8 got for her. She was so drunk at the time that he thinks she was not sensible of her death, as she made no resistance whatever. She and her mother were both lodgers of Hare's, and they were both of idle habits, and much given to drinking. This was the only murder that Burke committed by himself, but what Hare was connected with. She was laid with her face downwards, and he pressed her down, and she was soon suffocated.

There was a Mrs Hostler washing in John Broggan's, and she came back next day to finish up the clothes, and when done, Hare and Burke gave her some whisky to drink, which made her drunk. This was in the daytime. She then went to bed. Mrs Broggan was out at the time. Hare and Burke murdered her the same way they did the others, and put her in a box, and set her in the coal-house in the passage, and carried her off to Dr Knox's in the afternoon of the same day, and got £8 for her. Broggan's wife was out of the house at the time the murder was committed. Mrs Hostler had ninepence halfpenny in her hand, which they could scarcely get out of it after she was dead, so firmly was it grasped.

The woman Campbell or Docherty was murdered on the 31st October last, and she was the last one. Burke declares that Hare perjured himself on his trial, when giving his evidence against him, as the woman Campbell or Docherty lay down among some straw at the bedside, and Hare laid hold of her mouth and nose, and pressed her throat, and Burke assisted him in it, till she was dead. Hare was not sitting on a chair at the time, as he said in the Court. There were seven shillings in the woman's pocket, which were divided between Hare and Burke.

That was the whole of them—sixteen in whole: nine were murdered in Hare's house, and four in John Broggan's; two in Hare's stable, and one in Burke's brother's house in the Canongate. Burke declares that five of them were murdered in Hare's room that has the iron bolt in the inside of it. Burke did not know the days nor the months the different murders were committed, nor all their names. They were generally in a state of intoxication at those times, and paid little attention to them; but they were all from 12 February till 1st November 1828; but he thinks Dr Knox will know by the dates of paying him the money for them. He never was concerned with any other person but Hare in those matters, and was never a resurrection man, and never dealt in dead bodies but what he murdered. He was urged by Hare's wife to murder Helen McDougal, the woman he lived with. The plan was, that he was to go to the country for a few weeks, and then write to Hare that she had died and was buried, and he was to tell this to deceive the neighbours; but he would not agree to it. The reason was, they could not trust to her, as she was a Scotch woman. Helen McDougal and Hare's wife were not present when those murders were committed: they might have a suspicion of what was doing, but did not see them done. Hare was always the most anxious about them, and could sleep well at night after committing a murder; but Burke repented often of the crime, and could not sleep without a bottle of whisky by his bedside, and a twopenny candle to burn all night beside him; when he awoke he would take a draught of the bottle—sometimes half a bottle at a draught—and that would make him sleep.

They had a great many pointed out for murder, but were disappointed of them by some means or other; they were always in a drunken state when they committed those murders, and when they got the money for them while it lasted. When done, they would pawn their clothes, and would take them out as soon as they got a subject. When they first began this murdering system, they always took them to Knox's after dark; but being so successful, they went in the day-time, and grew more bold. When they carried the girl Paterson to Knox's, there were a great many boys in the High School Yards, who followed Burke and the man that carried her, crying, "They are carrying a corpse"; but they got her safe delivered. They often said to one another that no person could find them out, no one being present at the murders but themselves two; and that they might be as well hanged for a sheep as a lamb. They made it their business to look out for persons to decoy into their houses to murder them. Burke declares, when they kept the mouth and nose shut a very few minutes, they could make no resistance, but would convulse and make a rumbling noise in their bellies for some time; after they ceased crying and making resistance, they left them to die of themselves; but their bodies would often move afterwards, and for some time they would have long breathings before life went away. Burke declares that it was God's providence that put a stop to their murdering career, or he does not know how far they might have gone with it, even to attack people on the streets, as they were so successful, and always met with a ready market: that when they delivered a body they were always told to get more.

Hare was always with him when he went with a subject, and also when he got the money. Burke declares, that Hare and him had a plan made up, that Burke and a man were to go to Glasgow or Ireland, and try the same there, and to forward them to Hare, and he was to give them to Dr Knox. Hare's wife always got £1 of Burke's share, for the use of the house, of all that were murdered in their house; for if the price received was £10, Hare got £6, and Burke got only £4; but Burke did not give her the £1 for Daft Jamie, for which Hare's wife would not speak to him for three weeks. They could get nothing done during the harvest-time, and also after harvest, as Hare's house was so full of lodgers. In Hare's house were eight beds for lodgers; they paid 3d. each; and two, and sometimes three, slept in a bed; and during harvest they gave up their own beds when throng. Burke declares they went under the name of resurrection men in the West Port, where they lived, but not murderers. When they wanted money, they would say they would go and look for a shot; that was the name they gave them when they wanted to murder any person. They entered into a contract with Dr Knox and his assistants that they were to get £10 in winter, and £8 in summer for as many subjects as they could bring to them.

Old Donald, a pensioner, who lodged in Hare's house, and died of a dropsy, was the first subject they sold. After he was put into the coffin and the lid put on, Hare unscrewed the nails and Burke lifted the body out. Hare filled the coffin with bark from the tanyard, and put a sheet over the bark, and it was buried in the West Churchyard. The coffin was furnished by the parish. Hare and Burke took him to the College first; they saw a man there, and asked for Dr Monro, or any of his men; the man asked what they wanted, or had they a subject; they said they had. He then ordered them to call at 10 o'clock at Dr Knox's, in Surgeon Square, and he would take it from them, which they did. They got £7. 10s. for him. That was the only subject they sold that they did not murder; and getting that high price made them try the murdering for subjects.

Burke is 36 years of age, was born in the parish of Orrey, county Tyrone; served seven years in the army, most of that time as an officer's servant in the Donegal Militia; he was married at Ballinha, in the county of Mayo, when in the army, but left his wife and two children in Ireland. She would not come to Scotland with him. He has often wrote to her, but got no answer; he came to Scotland to work at the Union Canal, and wrought there while it lasted; he resided for about two years in Peebles, and worked as a labourer. He wrought as weaver for 18 months, and as a baker for five months; he learned to mend shoes, as a cobbler, with a man he lodged with in Leith; and he has lived with Helen McDougal about ten years, until he and she were confined in the Calton Jail, on the charge of murdering the woman of the name of Docherty or Campbell, and both were tried before the High Court of Justiciary in December last. Helen McDougal's charge was found not proven, and Burke found guilty, and sentenced to suffer death on the 28 January.

Declares, that Hare's servant girl could give information respecting the murders done in Hare's house, if she likes. She came to him at Whitsunday last, went to harvest, and returned back to him when the harvest was over. She remained until he was confined along with his wife in the Calton Jail. She then sold 21 of his swine for £3, and absconded. She was gathering potatoes in a field that day Daft Jamie was murdered; when saw his clothes in the house when she came home at night. Her name is Elizabeth McGuier or Mair. Their wives saw that people came into their houses at night, and went to bed as lodgers, but did not see them in the morning, nor did they make any inquiries after them. They certainly knew what became of them, although Burke and Hare pretended to the contrary. Hare's wife often helped Burke and Hare to pack the murdered bodies into the boxes. Helen M'Dougal never did, nor saw them done; Burke never durst let her know; he used to smuggle in drink, and get better victuals unknown to her; he told her he bought dead bodies, and sold them to doctors, and that was the way they got the name of resurrection-men.

Burk declares that Docter Knox never incoureged him, nither taught him or incoreged him to murder any person, nether any of his asistents, that worthy gentleman Mr Ferguson was the only man that ever mentioned any thing about the bodies. He inquired where we got that young woman Paterson.

(*Signed*) WILLIAM BURK, prisoner.

Bibliography

A very large number of pamphlets, broadsheets, cartoons, verses and songs appeared in Edinburgh and elsewhere between the discovery of the West Port murders in November 1828 and the end of 1829. Newspapers filled columns with details of the murderers and their victims, and a part-work was snapped up as soon as it appeared on the streets. Much more has been published on Burke and Hare since the end of the story in 1829, both fact and fiction, but there have been remarkably few serious attempts to examine the crimes and set them against their time. This list is not an exhaustive one; it is merely the principal works which have been of use to me in writing this book.

NEWSPAPERS AND PERIODICALS

Blackwood's Edinburgh Magazine
The Caledonian Mercury
The Edinburgh Advertiser
The Edinburgh Evening Courant
The Edinburgh Evening Dispatch
The Edinburgh Evening News
The Edinburgh Observer
The Edinburgh Weekly Chronicle
The Glasgow Chronicle
The New Scots Magazine
The Newcastle Chronicle
The Phrenological Journal

The Scotsman
Scottish Country Life
The Weekly Scotsman

BOOKS AND PAMPHLETS

Adam, Hargrave L., *Burke and Hare*, London, 1948
Atlay, J. B., *Famous Trials of the Century*, London, 1899
Bridie, James, *The Anatomist*, London, 1931
Bailey, J. B., *Diary of a Resurrectionist, 1811–12*, London, 1896
Brown, J. and G., *The Story of Daft Jamie: Reprint of A Laconic Narrative of the Life and Death of James Wilson, Known by the Name of Daft Jamie*, published by W. Smith, Edinburgh, 1829; Edinburgh, 1881
Buchanan, Robert (Publisher), *Trial of William Burke and Helen McDougal Before the High Court of Justiciary, at Edinburgh, on Wednesday, December 24, 1828, for the Murder of Margery Campbell or Docherty* (Based on the shorthand transcription of John Macnee, writer), Edinburgh, 1829
Burke, W., *Account of the Life of W.B.*, Cheap Tracts No. 16, Dunfermline, 1829
Caldwell, G. (Publisher), *A Correct Account of the Life, Confession, and Execution of William Burke, Who was Executed at Edinburgh, on Wednesday, 28th January, 1829*, Paisley, 1829
Cockburn, Henry, *Memorials of His Time*, Edinburgh, 1856
The Echo of Surgeons Square. Letter to The Lord Advocate Disclosing The Accomplices, Secrets and Other Facts Relative To The Late Murders; With A Correct Account Of The Manner In Which The Anatomical Schools Are Supplied With Subjects (Attributed to David Paterson), Edinburgh, 1829
High Court of Justiciary, Books of Adjournal 1828–29
High Court of Justiciary Minute Book, 1828–29
Hunter, R. H., *The Resurrectionists*, Belfast, 1925
Hunter, R. H., *Short History of Anatomy*, Belfast, 1931
Ireland, Thomas (Publisher), *West Port Murders; Or an Authentic Account of The Atrocious Murders Committed by Burke and his Associates, etc.*, 15 parts, Edinburgh, 1828–29

Leighton, Alexander, *The Court of Cacus*, Edinburgh, 1861

Lockhart, J. G., *Memoirs of the Life of Sir Walter Scott*, Edinburgh, 1837

Lonsdale, Henry, *A Sketch of the Life and Writings of Robert Knox, the Anatomist*, London, 1870

MacGregor, G., *The History of Burke and Hare and of Resurrection Times*, Glasgow, 1884

Nimmo, R. H. (Publisher), *Noxiana*, Edinburgh, 1829

Nimmo, R. H. (Publisher), *Wretch's Illustrations of Shakespeare*, Edinburgh, 1829

Rae, Isobel, *Knox, The Anatomist*, Edinburgh, 1964

Roughead, William, *The Trial of Burke and Hare*, Notable British Trials Series, Edinburgh, 1921

Scott, Sir Walter, *Journal*, Edinburgh, 1890

Sharp, Charles Kirkpatrick (Editor), *Trial of William Burke and Helen McDougal*, Edinburgh, 1829

Stevenson, R. L. "The Body Snatcher", *Pall Mall Gazette Christmas Extra*, 1884

Stone, Thomas, *Observations On The Phrenological Development of Burke, Hare, And Other Atrocious Murderers, etc*, Edinburgh, 1829

Syme, David, *Reports of Proceedings in the High Court of Justiciary from 1826–1829*, Edinburgh, 1829

Thomas, Dylan, *The Doctor and the Devils*, London, 1953

Waugh, Mansie, *Mansie Waugh's Dream Concerning the Execution of Burke*, Edinburgh, 1829

Index

O

Ostler, Mrs, 49, 133, 134, 135, 170, 179

P

Paterson, David (*see also Echo of Surgeons' Square*), 35, 44, 45, 50, 56, 61, 62, 63, 69, 79, 84, 108, 109, 110, 157, 173, 178
——, Elizabeth, 79
Paterson (or Mitchell), Mary, 41–5, 52, 70, 71, 72, 99, 102, 109, 110, 132, 133, 134, 135, 159, 161, 163, 164, 170, 175, 181, 183
Pattison, Granville Sharp, 27
Patton, George, 76
Pitmilly, Lord, 76, 77, 115

Q

Queensberry, Marquis of, 138
Quincey, Thomas de, 157, 158

R

Rae, Sir William (Lord Advocate), 71, 72, 76, 77, 78, 79, 83, 84, 85, 86, 88, 89, 90, 91, 93, 98, 105, 111, 112, 115, 116, 125, 130, 149
Rea, William, 26
Reid, Father William, 104, 105, 118, 119, 172
Robertson, Patrick, 76, 77
Rymer's Shop, 51, 54, 59, 60, 63, 87, 132, 177

S

Sandford, Ernest Douglas, 116, 127
Scott, Archibald (Procurator Fiscal), 105, 166
——, Sir Walter, 14, 106, 122, 136, 138, 157

Simpson, Abigail, 38–9, 40, 131, 133, 134, 135, 167, 168, 173
'Spune' (resurrectionist), 23, 24
Stevenson, Robert Louis, 158, 159
Stewart, Mary, 78, 79
'Stupe' (resurrectionist), 123
Surgeons, Royal College of (Edinburgh), 19, 142
——, Royal College of (London), 147, 148, 153
——, Royal College of (Dublin), 25, 26
Surgeons' Square, No 10, 17, 35, 37, 38, 40, 44, 45, 48, 49, 50, 51, 52, 55, 65, 66, 67, 69, 79, 80, 89, 104, 120, 132, 178
Surtees, R. S., 157
Swanston's Tavern, 42, 44, 102
Syme, James, 18

T

Tait, George (Sheriff Substitute), 67, 104, 114, 126, 166
Tanner's Close (Hares' lodging house), 39, 41, 46, 47, 49, 50, 51, 55, 60, 71, 99, 132, 135, 180, 181, 183
Thomas, Dylan, 159

W

Warburton, Henry, 147, 154
Williams, Thomas, 151, 152, 153
Wilson, 'Daft Jamie', 52–6, 70, 71, 72, 95, 99, 100, 102, 110, 114, 116, 120, 125, 132, 133, 134, 136, 161, 162, 170, 177, 178, 181, 183
——, Mrs Janet, 52, 112, 116, 125, 126, 178
——, Miss Janet, 114, 116, 125, 126
Wood, Alexander, 76, 87
Wretch's Illustrations from Shakespeare, 100